BEATS ME

MARYROSE CARROLL

Also by Maryrose Carroll
Alice's Book;
Variations on a Theme of Lewis Carroll's
TriQuarterly Press, 1982

About Maryrose Carroll

The artist and writer Maryrose Carroll was married to the poet and teacher Paul Carroll from 1977 until his death in 1996. BEATS ME offers insights into literature and the literary life she learned through conversations they had and through meeting Saul Bellow, William Burroughs, Allen Ginsberg, Studs Terkel, Pete Seeger, and many others who played a role in Paul's writing and editing career.

BEATS ME

Love, Poetry, Censorship

from

Chicago to Appalachia

Maryrose Carroll

With an Introduction by Joseph Bathanti

"A Preface for Paul" by Lawrence Ferlinghetti

Edited by Nora Percival and Dan Campion

 BIG TABLE BOOKS

2053 Beaver Dam Road
North Carolina 28692
www.BigTableBook.com

Library of Congress Control Number 2015900842
ISBN 978-0-692-36992-0

The author gratefully acknowledges permission to reprint material from the following sources:

Cover photo of Paul Carroll and Allen Ginsberg, 1958, Paul D. Carroll Papers, Special Collections Research Center, University of Chicago Library.

Interior sketch of Paul Carroll at the Cape Cod Room, Chicago, June Leaf, New York, New York.

Back Cover, "A Life in Beat Poetics," Glenn A. Bruce, http://the beatpoetsoftheforevergenera.blogspot.com

"We walk inside the heart of God all day."
"Psalm 3," *Poems & Psalms*, Paul Carroll. 1927 -1996

Beats Me

Table of Contents

Introduction

Blue Smoke

"For a while I used to see colors inside of people and once, when Paul had rested from writing, I could see blue smoke rising from his head."

- Maryrose Carroll

On Valentine's Day, 2013, I gave a reading of my work at the Watauga County Public Library in Boone, North Carolina, where I live and work. Maryrose Carroll, though I didn't know her at the time, was in the audience. After the reading, a discussion ensued. A number of the poems I had read were about the working-class Italian immigrant laborers I had grown up among. My parents – my father, a steelworker, my mother a seamstress – figure largely in my work. Maryrose remarked how crucial it was to have poetry of witness that champions the common people, that poetry at its most powerful, at its democratic pinnacle, champions the stories of the common people. She cited Latin American culture where poetry is the substance of the everyday, not simply the possession of the intelligentsia. Pablo Neruda, she testified, had gone into the Chilean coal mines and crouched there inside the earth among the miners. As I listened, I wondered who this extraordinary woman was, though I habitually run into unassuming brilliant people in libraries – places that remain, I pray, safe havens to talk about the things one loves and are sustained by.

At any rate, a handful of people were kind enough after discussion to walk forward and speak to me. One of them was Maryrose: pretty, a bit older than I, confident, clear-eyed, erect, and wearing an exquisite scarf. She proffered one of my books. When I asked to whom I should inscribe it, she said, "Maryrose." Then it all clicked. I felt a little pang, and a great rush of humility, and then utterly delighted that I was looking at her and had just had her hand in mine. She was Maryrose Carroll. I want to say next that she is Paul Carroll's wife, and she is, married to him from 1977 until his death in 1996. But I'm hesitant to qualify her in that fashion, though I doubt she'd mind. She was and is a clearly defined presence of her own, "a figure of central interest and importance in the great efflorescence of American sculpture," as one of her bios states. Her massive public sculptures tower in North Carolina cities like Charlotte, Hickory, and Fayetteville. They are also in Illinois and California, in museums in Chicago and Springfield, in Hartford and Dayton. She has taught at Northwestern University and Appalachian State University. I was honored, astonished, to meet her, and we have been friends ever since.

Paul Carroll is an acknowledged, major figure in the avant-garde movement of poetry in the middle twentieth century. He is identified with the canonical Black Mountain Poets as well as the Beats. He's featured prominently in Donald Allen's groundbreaking 1960 anthology *The New American Poetry*, published by Grove Press. Carroll lines up in the volume, its cover an American flag, with a decidedly exclusive club: Robert Creeley, Robert Duncan, Denise Levertov, Allen Ginsberg, Charles Olson, and many other venerable poets of this generation. He founded the Poetry Center of Chicago, was the poetry editor of *Chicago Review* and also a cofounder and editor of *Big Table*.

Paul and Maryrose met in 1977 at a Chicago art gallery. A week later, Paul proposed. When he retired from the University of Illinois at Chicago, in 1993, they moved to a farmhouse (only the third family to live there since 1897) in the Bethel community, in North Carolina, ten miles or so out of Boone, in far western Watauga County, verging on Tennessee, deep in the Appalachian Mountains, where Maryrose still resides with her horses. Paul Carroll is interred in the columbarium at Saint Elizabeth's of the Hill Country Catholic Church in Boone. A dogwood blooms just above the creek stonewall of the columbarium and the terse epitaph: *Paul Carroll, 1927– 1996.*

Maryrose Carroll's memoir, *Beats Me: Love, Poetry, Censorship from Chicago to Appalachia,* is a love story – and, in the bargain, a fascinating account of some of the most vibrant, stormy and controversial times in American literature. In fact, for any student of twentieth-century poetry, it's downright mesmerizing.

Paul Carroll took over as guest poetry editor of *Chicago Review* in 1957. An essay of his, "Notes on Some Young Poets," published in the *Review*, published that same year, indicted what he called the "young gray-flannel poet," and sent out the call for new poets, new voices, to supplant the "soporific and enervated work" he found all too prevalent at the time. To drum up "new voices," Carroll approached Lawrence Ferlinghetti, and soon he was in possession of manuscripts from Allen Ginsberg, William Burroughs, and Jack Kerouac – the Beat Trinity, if you will. In fact, it was Ginsberg who suggested *Chicago Review* publish excerpts of Burroughs's explosive, inscrutable *Naked Lunch.*

Carroll and fellow *Chicago Review* editor Irving Rosenthal went ahead and indeed published excerpts of

Naked Lunch in what they called the San Francisco issue, accompanied by work by Kerouac, Ginsberg, and Robert Duncan. This issue along with the following issue on Zen Buddhism became the best-selling issues in the history of the magazine. Sales tripled. The fallout, however, was profound. *The Chicago Daily News* ran a story on its front page – "Filthy Writing on the Midway" – not only vilifying the editors of *Chicago Review,* but calling into question the integrity of the University of Chicago for supporting such obscenity. The university caved in under the uproar and forbade Carroll and Rosenthal from publishing the next issue, which was to feature additional excerpts from *Naked Lunch.*

Rosenthal resigned as editor and, shortly thereafter, so did Carroll. Out of this furor over censorship was born *Big Table,* a very short-lived, but legendary magazine. Its very first issue, published in March of 1959, contained the suppressed *Chicago Review* material, including additional excerpts from *Naked Lunch,* and portions of Kerouac's *Old Angel Midnight.* That inaugural issue was impounded by the U. S. Post Office for "obscenity and filthy contents." Eventually a court ruled in favor of *Big Table,* but not without a considerable battle – the history of which is painstakingly documented by Maryrose Carroll. Included, as well, is a priceless monologue of Paul's wherein he recapitulates the glory of publishing the five issues that comprised the entirety of *Big Table*'s life span from 1959 to 1961. In addition to those already mentioned, *Big Table* published Ferlinghetti, Gregory Corso, Robert Duncan, Paul Blackburn, John Logan, Frank O'Hara, Edward Dahlberg, Paul Bowles, Kenneth Koch, John Ashbery, Pablo Neruda, John Updike, Norman Mailer, James Wright, and many others.

Ginsberg, especially, gets a lot of play in *Beats Me*. He shows up again and again and there's a wonderful scene, recalled by Maryrose, when he presents her and Paul with a signed copy of "Howl" and kisses her "smack on [her] lips." She also recounts Paul saying that he "didn't mind [Ginsberg] sticking his tongue in [his] ear...," but when Ginsberg ventures advice on how Carroll should write poetry, Carroll hurls a whiskey glass at him that "[breaks] against a wall, missing both Allen and a Jackson Pollock painting." The book is filled with these kinds of fireworks (and it's worth mentioning, as well, that there are cameos by the likes of Mike Nichols, Studs Terkel, Pete Seeger, James Dickey; and a thorough reflection on Saul Bellow). Indeed, Ginsberg – as a kind of totem for the fight against censorship in mid-twentieth-century America = informs this book in significant ways.

Beats Me is essential reading for Beat aficionados. It's also a tour de force of *Big Table* and like-minded, cutting-edge journals that attempted, often under duress, to move outside the established circles of poetry of that era. *Beats Me* is an unforgettable record of the pivotal moments in the mid-twentieth century when a handful of fire-breathing writers and editors, like Paul Carroll, refused to buckle under censorship. In his preface to the selection of Paul's poems in this volume, Lawrence Ferlinghetti calls Paul Carroll "one of the great counter-culture poetry editors."

I could certainly go on and dig in further on this trove of captivating lore that Maryrose so beautifully trots out, but what I've reported here is a mere précis of the invaluable scholarly and archival importance that *Beats Me* spills over with -- not to mention an extensive bibliography and a generous sampling of Paul Carroll's poems and poem fragments that follow Maryrose's recollection.

This is a wonderful book. It will have readers divining blue smoke.

 • Joseph Bathanti

Acknowledgments

My first book, *Alice's Book,* a tribute to Lewis Carroll, consisted of my photographs and his verse. As *Beats Me* was written and not photographed, it took a whole army to help me march it to completion. I could not conceive of finishing this book without my editors Nora Percival and Dan Campion. There was a whole band of cheerleaders encouraging this project starting with Joseph Potter, and including Myron Ball, Johanna Hays, Ann Gonzalez, Peggy Poe Stern, Ree Strawser, Jeff Block, John Higby, Tom McGowan, Glenn A. Bruce, Will Morgan, Betsy Willis, and Rick Kogan.

Then my fellow members of High Country Writers, Judy Geary and Anita Laymon added their publishing expertise. In the case of this book it took a village to enable a fledgling writer.

I will always be grateful to Alice Schreyer at the University of Chicago Library for her direction in establishing the archiving of Paul D. Carroll's Papers at the Special Collections Research Center at the University of Chicago Library and for our friendship of sixteen years.

June Leaf, my husband's dear love before my turn came, did what only an excellent artist can do, capture spontaneously the image of Paul's intensity and vitality on the back of an envelope while they were dining at the Cape Cod Room in Chicago.

Joseph Bathanti, a dear friend and the seventh Poet Laureate of North Carolina, generously offered his poetic insight for the introduction to *Beats Me.* Lawrence Ferlinghetti was kind enough to write his feelings in A Preface for Paul, about a pal and his legacy.

Without Paul Carroll, Big Table, this book, and *Big*

Table Book Publishing would not exist and my life would have not sparkled.

I hope you, dear reader, will enjoy this book.

Preface

Combining literary history with very personal drama I tell the tale of my husband, Paul Carroll, and his exploits with censorship by the University of Chicago of writings by Jack Kerouac, Allen Ginsberg, and William S. Burroughs, which subsequently were published in the little magazine, *Big Table*. The U.S. Post Office then attempted to censor the same writings in 1959. His stories, told to me nightly, progress like Scheherazade's, through the course of the last year of his life, when he learns he is dying from cancer.

His wounded friendship with Allen Ginsberg evolves over the course of three decades. Allen is pivotal in the first publishing of excerpts of *Naked Lunch* in *Big Table* but dictatorial in his direction of how Paul should write his poetry. Paul's verse evolves over thirty years from the highly structured Sicilian sestet of "Winter Scene" published in 1958 in the *New Yorker* to the immediacy of late lines as:

"'We walk inside the heart of God all day.'"

The history continues in 1968 with Paul's partnership with Follett Publishing Co. to produce *Big Table Books,* including *The Poem In Its Skin* and *Young American Poets,* which Kenneth Clarke, when director of the Poetry Center of Chicago founded by Paul, called "the bible."

A great friendship starts with James Dickey in 1959, who described his visits with Paul in Chicago as "I do sincerely believe that was the happiest I ever was in my life. The happiest."

Dickey's and Paul's friendship involved a mutual appreciation and respect for each other's poetry and Jim's last letter, written after Paul's death, said, "I hope you will continue to stay in touch so that we may be with Paul on both sides of the shadow line. One can do such things, as you know." Well, I didn't know that at the time of his letter, but I was to find out he was correct.

Communication can continue with a loved one after their death.

An Epiphany

"How much longer did Dr. DeVirgilis say I have?"

I turn to stare at my husband, his tall figure diminished by leaning back in his chair with his arms crossed behind his head. The sun through the window bounces off his balding brow. His baritone clarified by years of giving readings is low and breathy as he turns to me and asks his question again.

"How much longer did Dr. DeVirgilis say I have?"

I have an answer, even though there isn't one. How long is a year if it's your last year?

"Plenty of time, Paul, to fill in the gaps and get into my memory everything you think is important to you. Why don't you begin by reminding me how you started writing?"

As I sat listening to Paul's life that I wanted so much to preserve, I was both scribe and lover. As scribe, not knowing how rapidly the cancer was taking over his body, I wanted to catch his every word. As lover, it was Paul himself I wanted to preserve.

"Posey, are you really interested in that ancient history? We could talk about our neighbors, or the

Baptists, or sex."

"C'mon honey, I want the story of how the love of your life grabbed you. I know you love me, but it's writing that you've romanced every day for the last, what – fifty years?"

"I guess it's that long. Have another sip of wine and relax, kid. You know I'm not stingy with words."

Settling in my chair beside his rosewood desk I realize how healthy he appears.

"Is it hot outside?" he asks.

"No, dear. The wind coming up the valley has cooled the air. Would you like some wine?"

"You know the answer. My love, as you say, for literature began in college. Until one Saturday afternoon, I was an average Joe going through school on the GI bill, chasing ladies, playing basketball, drifting like a rudderless dinghy on a pond."

"It's hard for me to imagine you coasting, Paul. Every day, every single bloody day you write and rewrite into the wee small hours."

"Yea, I was a different person then. My service, the end of the war, was really easy and afterward I had no idea of what to do with my life. So I followed friends to college at Illinois Wesleyan University. Can you imagine me attending a daily Protestant service? My family, living or dead, would shudder. It was my difficulty with my German class, hard for me to understand, that became the catapult to writing. I have been fluent in Latin since my days at Catholic grammar and high school. Nevertheless I had trouble correctly pronouncing such a heavy language as German. Who else in the world but Germans would say *Ich liebe dich* when they mean 'I love you?'

"Imagine a romantic moonlit night, reflections on the water, a soft breeze tickling the trees, then I turn to you and say *Ich liebe dich*. You might say – 'Do what to your dick? I've always wondered if German lovers were less passionate than the Italians or the French – being hindered by their native tongue."

"Paul, I don't think I've ever read a dissertation on that subject."

"Elsa was a wholesome, handsome young woman who offered to help me with my German; so I asked her out on a date."

"Paul, this leads to your budding interest in

literature?"

"Patience, patience, please."

"It was a Saturday afternoon and I had picked up my best trousers from the dry cleaners. As I headed back to my dorm with them over my arm, a heavy rain started to fall, so I ducked into the library to keep them dry. Since the rain didn't promise to end quickly I tried to think what I could do to pass the time there.

"At that time in my life going to a library was as foreign to me as joining the French Foreign Legion. All I could think of was the rumor I heard in communications class that a book called *Ulysses* by James Joyce had some racy parts. I promise this is leading somewhere.

"I approached the librarian and asked for *Ulysses*. She told me I would need a note from a professor because, until recently, the book had been banned for obscenity. Thinking I must be on the right track, I retreated to an obscure corner and sat down and wrote a note from Elsa's father, Professor Schmidt, saying I was authorized to borrow a copy of *Ulysses*. Fortunately, the librarian bought my forgery.

"I began to read this famous novel and on the first

page I found a familiar Latin phrase, '*Introibo ad altar Dei*' (I go up to the altar of God). I thought, of course, he's Irish. A few pages later I read, '*Woodshadows floated silently by through the morning peace from the stairhead seaward where he gazed. Inshore and farther out the mirror of water whitened, spurned by lightshod hurrying feet. White breast of the dim sea. The twining stresses, two by two. A hand plucking the harpstrings merging their twining chords. Wavewhite wedded words shimmering on the dim tide.*'

"Honey, I couldn't understand what I'd just read. '*Wavewhite wedded words.* "Is it prose or poetry? How do these words seem to gather resonance and mesmerize me? I felt like I had dropped down a rabbit hole. And as I leaned back my trousers slid off the other chair and onto the floor. This book had knocked my pants off! I searched ahead for racy bits but didn't find any. With a change in the sounds outside I realized the weather was letting up. In the years since that afternoon I had come to realize that this experience was, as Carlos Castaneda says, 'a knock on my consciousness.' Joyce's words had hit something unknown in my psyche, an unknown part of me. Soon I forgot about sweethearts, my classes; basketball. All I wanted to do was read. My future -- think of this, Posie -- hinged on an unexpected arrival of rain.

"From this point forward, I began to see my future. But I didn't know yet that writing poetry, attending the University of Chicago, meeting Allen Ginsberg, were all ahead of me. Is it karma, providence, or divine will which controls us?

"The weather had changed outside the library and inside my head. I had a date to get to that evening but within a day or so I realized there was a much more important date for me to make."

"Paul, you're weary and happy. Let's call it an evening. Just look out the window, at the half moon shining so brightly in the indigo sky."

To *"Labour by singing light"*

It was our ritual here on the farm in Appalachia, and for years back in Chicago, to meet before the sunset to share our day's events and play with our puppy, Kayo. For Paul these events were his new poems. You see, James Joyce had taken Paul by the hand to lead him forward to a celebrated life as a poet and the principal actor in a fight against literary censorship. Our long-standing routine would now be changed to accommodate his new role as Scheherazade, nightly telling his history: a role I dearly hoped would last at least a full year.

When we lived in Chicago, when Paul wasn't teaching he would sail out on his bike, leaving behind the noise and grime of our Ada Street loft, heading for Lincoln Park to write his poetry. It was because of this exercise, sometimes biking twenty miles a day, that Paul had Lance Armstrong legs and seemed fit despite his smoking and drinking.

Before meeting Paul, I had bought half a warehouse for the unbelievable price of fourteen thousand dollars, enabling me to live in the city while working on my sculpture. What a miracle! Only three miles from the John

Hancock Center on North Michigan Avenue, the Ada Street loft was set in a triangle of abandoned manufacturing plants bordered by the Chicago River and Elston Avenue (one of those few arteries to cut diagonally across the grid of Chicago's streets). U.S. Steel had left. Proctor and Gamble would soon follow.

My half of the warehouse had previously held loose charcoal. It took three days to hose it out. The other owner, my partner John Henry, had offices in the front area with dozens of phone connections. It had probably been a bookie joint at one time. A two-minute walk would take me to Sax's restaurant, The Hideout, where breakfast and lunch were served to businessmen who drove ten minutes from the Loop to escape their offices. I can remember eating lunch, watching a ball game, when the phone would ring. Sax would pick it up, listen to the caller, and then ask, "Is Winkler here?" Winkler, sitting two seats away, would shake his head no and Sax would mutter "NO" into the receiver.

Three years after I bought my portion of the building, Paul and I met by chance at an African art exhibition at the Richard Gray Gallery. Within two months we were married in a ceremony conducted by one of his former students, Paul Hoover, who had a ministerial degree. In his youth Paul had been used to high-toned luxury living. When he moved in with me, in 1977, partnering love with no rent, it was also an incredible act of accommodation on

Paul and Maryrose Carroll on honeymoon in San Francisco, 1977

his part. One of his dedicated poetry students, Peter Kostakis, helped us move Paul's things to Ada Street. The only similarities between Ada Street and the Appalachian farm we moved to next, besides the letter A, were that the sun shone on both and there was running water nearby. At

Ada Street, trying our best we could only see three stars at night and the Chicago River did not make sweet music. I remember one night when a barge slammed into a dock, waking us up to the realization that all the power was off. Rats were more frequently sighted than birds, and six mornings a week we would wake at six to the rumble and tremor of steel traveling on a bridge crane in the factory next door. The paint factory on the other side exuded a toxic stink. Besides all this Paul would have to contend with my sculpture noise: cutting, grinding, welding, aluminum. No wonder my poor poet would take off on his bike to get away to find a quiet place to write.

While in pursuit of poetic ambush (his phrase) he would bike until fresh lines, waiting behind a tree or bush, grabbed his attention. Then, opening his backpack and pushing aside a can of tuna and a tomato, he would pull out his lined yellow notebook and pen and would, as he said, write madly like a scribe.

Having captured fresh game, whether an idea, or a few lines, he would remount his bike until being ambushed again. Once he returned from his hunt, he would nap and then begin to edit what he had caught. Later, usually around three, in the dead of night while I was fast asleep, he would resume his editing. Paul's sunset reciting was of poems new that day, or previously written and now edited. A constant, prodigious regime of writing poetry had developed from the unexpected rain that drove him into the library years ago.

From that huge, cold, and grimy Chicago warehouse loft we moved to a hundred-year-old farmhouse surrounded by horses, fields, trees, and mountain ridges framing a narrow valley: from urban blight to heaven. That was after Paul retired as a Professor Emeritus from the University of Illinois at Chicago, in 1993. (This honor wouldn't have happened if Don Marshall had not become the new Department of English Chairman. He successfully shielded Paul from the envy of other professors in the department.)

When we moved here, Paul and I became the first resident non-Ellers. They were the extended family that built and occupied this house, for one hundred years. Our property is tucked in the eastern face of the last ridge before the Stone Mountains, which create the state line between North Carolina and Tennessee. Our Little Beaver

Dam Creek, fronting the public side of the farm, feeds into Beaver Dam Creek and then the Watauga River. During the Tennessee Valley Authority development in the 1940s it was the building of the Watauga Dam that brought electricity to this area while burying Butler, Tennessee, under water.

When the weather is kind, Paul and I love to move out from the house to sit under the Chinese chestnut trees framing the creek to sip our wine and talk. He says the creek sometimes sounds like jazzman Bix Beiderbecke's cornet.

Tonight the early evening sky is soft and clear. Paul can easily walk this far, so I go by the creek and set up our chairs, spread a cloth over the table, and bring out a tray with wine and glasses. He slowly lowers his 178 pounds into a wicker seat, sighing with relief and reaching down to pet Kayo.

"Posie, I don't have my usual energy," he admits.

"I know you don't, honey." Neither of us says cancer like a silent thief in the night is stealing it away.

Sipping from his wine, Paul leans backward in his seat, gazes around, then turns and looks at me with an intense, almost fierce focus while he asks, "Will I ever see you, or touch your soft face again, when death hauls me out of this world? Just the thought of leaving you stabs – at my heart – stops it beating. You have propped me up, over and over. I feel like a traitor leaving you behind."

"Oh honey, I don't want to lose you either, but, Paul, this isn't anything we can fix."

Paul's doctor had told us that over many years smoking had deposited arsenic in his bladder. As a result, he now has cancer, which has spread to the nearby lymph nodes. Dr. DeVirgilis said there isn't a damned thing we can do to save his life. Whatever we could try, chemotherapy, radiation, surgery – would only cause grief. His final diagnosis was that Paul had about one year to live.

I touch his shoulder and tell him softly, "Paul, you are not a traitor. We will continue to love each other spending our time on what we can do in this year. You have to tell me everything, including the history you always resist – *Big Table* censorship."

Since he has fallen silent, I begin to think to myself; are we now free-falling toward death? What is death? Do I have any recollection? If I ever died before, I certainly don't remember it. Is there an afterlife, one outside space and time where he will eternally abide? Will Paul fly there with his satchel full of bright little nuggets of truth and passion, enduring all trials, and once there, merge with the consciousness of other spirits locked in a dance of love? Perhaps he will exist in the interstices between living and dead matter, sitting as an observer, or does he simply pass through the last sleep to an eternal void? Is it possible that there is nothing, instead of an eternal life? No matter how hard I try, I can't imagine that.

At least providence is giving him a year to ponder what his final words will be, whether these are chiseled in stone, or simply whispered in my ear, the wife who has lovingly shared his dreams, poems, and daily rituals for the last twenty years.

Suddenly he sits upright, breaking his silence. With renewed spirit he announces, "What I would like most to do this last year is make endless love with you. Please would you read a few lines from one of my poems?"

I pick up his well-used notebook from the table, and while he listens, I read:

SONG AFTER MAKING LOVE
Blood feels sweet
as if moving in maple trees
a part of me is grass
I close my eyes
I'm empty
at the same time full
like a galaxy in daylight

As I finish reading this section, Paul says, "Damn it, our sexy fun is being stolen by this goddamn cancer eating away at me." He pauses pensively, then adds, "What I can leave you are the stories of what I have done – my history, writing, love for you, Luke, and the poets I've known. You have heard so many of these, maybe too many times; about my Irish family, other writers. Do you still have patience to meet me at sunset, sharing wine and poetry? Ever since we met you have been my best audience, fan, and critic. After dinner, let's spend time together while I tell you what I think is worth preserving."

Holding Paul's hand, I say, "Paul your stories just can't stop while you can still speak. Absolutely, I want to hear everything you feel is important. Yes, please let's do this together."

"Honey, I knew you'd agree. Finally, I'll take the time to relate what I've been avoiding, sidestepping for thirty-five years, the complete story of *Big Table* magazine. And I'll add more memories of Allen Ginsberg– and other writers you have met."

"I've always wondered why you avoid talking about the Beat writers you published," I say.

"Well, you will finally know," he says, lowering his head with a sigh. "But not tonight, I'm tired, honey. Cancer is a damn stingy bastard; it's stealing all my energy. Posie, please help me get up."

"Where's Kayo?" he asks.

"He's eating his dinner in the spring house."

"Good! I hear coyotes barking up on the mountain. Two deaths in one year would be too much."

Brother Ferlinghetti

The next evening plinking of hard rain on the metal roof pushed us to the quiet side – Paul's office. As he sits there at his desk, dressed casually, yet stylish in his dark green corduroy trousers, ochre suede vest, and hound's-tooth newsboy cap, he observes: "This isn't bad wine," placing his glass on a coaster. "It's a bit sweet – hmm –not bad."

"Honey, it's organic and cheap. I don't think I could find anything better."

"Well, kid, here's a toast to your find. Fortunately, cancer hasn't caused me any pain, so I hope alcohol will be my only medication maybe until the end. Here's to life, all of it, anywhere, anytime," he said, raising his glass high.

After a long sip he returned it to the coaster, cleared his throat, and said:

"Here's what I have of a new poem. I'm calling it "A Virgilian Moon.""

A VIRGILIAN MOON

Abruptly,

The round moon blazes, white

As bone, alone

In a dark sky. The ancients were right –

The moon's a woman

And if I knew the words I'd pray to her tonight

In gratitude for my wife asleep

Whose body is another sky

Like the softness and the secrets of a summer's night.

"Oh, Paul. That's exquisite!" I said, leaning back on the sofa, hugging myself. "You write such beautiful love poetry, so delightful. I can't wait to hear the whole poem. Tell me, when you say Virgilian Moon, do you mean the moon is a guide, as Virgil was for Dante?"

"No, not really. Virgil was Dante's guide through hell and purgatory. I'm alluding to the way he talks about the moon being brighter than the brightest star, Hesperus."

"Ah, the incredible brilliance of light!"

Even with cancer Paul is still walking, and when we finish our wine he walks to the dining table in the next room without my help. He sits down and I serve him a bowl of soup.

"Maryrose, what's this shitty soup?"

"It's steak, dear, blended ground-up steak and onions with mushrooms. I hope you like it."

"Well, I'll give it a try," he says, tentatively. "The tomatoes on the side look nice but what's this? Banana pudding? Oh Christ, pretty soon you'll probably be serving me baby food."

"Oh, come on, Paul! But don't you get tired of spaghetti and sloppy joes?"

Despite new dentures and cancer, Paul still has a good appetite. Finishing his banana pudding, he says, "You know, that isn't a bad meal. But where's the wine? Do we have any left?"

With dinner finished I carried the bottle of wine to Paul's study, a south-side room in our white clapboard farmhouse. We are only the third family to live here since 1897, following two generations of the Eller family. They built this house from local wood they cut and then milled out in the yard.

Settled in his seat, Paul opened a drawer and took out a simple brass incense holder. He lit a cone of sandalwood, and its smoke wafted slowly toward the ceiling. He reached into his desk drawer and extracted what is, unmistakably, a cigarette stub.

My eyes opened wide. "Paul, what is that?"

"What does it look like, kid? It's a third of a ciggy. Be realistic! What difference can smoking make now? I'm dying. I can't just suddenly give it up. Not after fifty-six years. My strategy is to smoke only one cigarette a day by dividing it into thirds. One section for the morning, one for the afternoon, the last at night."

"Oh Christ! What can I say, Paul? You're probably right. How could it hasten your death? I know how much pleasure it gives you." I sigh again, sitting down, thinking how lucky I was never to get hooked by tobacco.

Paul studies me between puffs.

"You've never smoked, dear. You have no idea how it attaches itself to a person like a barnacle to a whale. My addiction comes partly from the message, the high, nicotine sends to my brain. The first smoke of the morning seems to clarify and focus my mind. Of course, I associate smoking with sex. Just think, Posie, how many times, lying beside you, basking in the after-pleasure of our lovemaking, I pulled out a Lucky Strike."

I thought: yes, I remember, you bet. When we are one body rolling together on our bed, beginning the inevitable slower tempo moving into quieter but still passionate embraces, our bodies side by side in these tender moments.

Paul sighed, "Fortunately, you don't know how lighting a cigarette enhances and prolongs my pleasure."

As he finished his cigarette he started to tease me. "What if, love, I haunt you after I die? Slip in while you are sleeping and cuddle by your side?"

"Well, I don't know, dear," joining his game. "The thought has never occurred to me. Will you be cold to touch?"

"Love, since there's no handbook on dying and the afterlife, we'll just have to wait and see. I think I've exhausted this cigarette, as well as the subject."

Slowly shaking my head, I asked: "Have you decided yet where to start in telling your stories? Do you want to start with *Big Table*?"

"No, actually I don't, although I probably should."

"Paul, why have you always shied away from talking about the censorship? Was it that painful?"

"Yes, in a way it was. At that time of my life, thirty-two, I had gotten my Masters in English Literature from the University of Chicago, published poems and a book translating the satirical letters of St. Jerome – not exactly Beat material. I had lectured at Notre Dame, the University of Chicago and Loyola University. Does that sound like a Beat? Actually, I probably appeared quite conventional. Also I had been poetry editor of the *Chicago Review* in 1950–52 and had just been asked again to be its guest poetry editor in 1957."

He passed a large black-and-white photo from 1959 to me and asked, "What do you see, dear?"

I was looking at a tall, lean young man with a crew cut: he was wearing tortoise-shell-rimmed glasses, a white shirt, a vest and wingtip shoes. Behind him was an antique rocking horse. He was right. He didn't look like a Beat. He looked like a confident intelligent man on the go, who listened to Studs Terkel's counsel: "Take it easy, but take it!

"So," I asked, "did the censorship and your association with Beats start at the *Chicago Review*?"

"Posie, you got it!"

"OK, Paul, so you jumped from translating letters by one of the Christian Church doctors to publishing renegade writers? That's quite a leap."

"Well, later I said I would even publish something by Richard Milhous Nixon, if it was good."

Paul Carroll, 1961. Photographed by Arthur Siegel.

"Paul, just how did this Beat connection come about?"

"Honey, it started with David Ray. In 1957 he was editor of the *Chicago Review* and he invited me back to be guest poetry editor. It was a student publication and though I had graduated a few years before, I continued to have a presence at the University of Chicago. Many of my early poems were published in the *Chicago Review*. David's successor was Irving Rosenthal, a psychology student, who asked me to continue as 'guest poetry editor.'"

"Paul, explain how Irving Rosenthal became the editor? I heard he wasn't a writer."

"Well, Irving started out as a student associate, a sometimes mind-numbing job reading dozens of submitted manuscripts. Then he wrote a story, 'An Invitation to Sleep', that Ray liked; so he gave his job to Irving when he stepped down.

"When Irving asked me to continue as 'guest poetry editor' we didn't know this was 'the beginning of a historic and controversial series of events which began with such a simple aim.' Irving and I just wanted to publish exciting new writing. We were looking for work we couldn't find in other little magazines such as *Accent, Partisan Review, Hudson Review,* and *Evergreen.* "My essay, 'Notes on Some Young Poets' which appeared in the autumn 1957 issue of the *Chicago Review,* called for new poetry to replace 'the soporific and enervated' work currently being published. I used the expression 'young gray-flannel poet' to describe most contemporary writers. I probably belonged in that category myself with my older work."

"What kind of writing were you looking for, Paul?"

"Simple. Anything that wasn't boring. I wrote to Lawrence Ferlinghetti, a poet and bookseller in San Francisco, to see if he had any names to suggest. I explained that the *Chicago Review* was interested in devoting an issue to San Francisco writers, and I hoped he would be our avenue in contacting them. He gave us Allen Ginsberg, who responded 'like a mad bibliographic scholar' and advised us to write to William S. Burroughs.

Lawrence was the middleman for these unique authors who would become known as Beats, and Irving and myself. Lawrence had said more than once: I am not a Beat. An orphan who grew to be exemplary in everything he did [Eagle Scout, World War II hero, doctorate from the University of Paris] he was handsome as well. In early 1950 he started a bookstore, City Lights, still in business today. Lawrence had conviction and balls. In 1957, arrested by city police, he went to jail for the publication of Allen Ginsberg's poem "Howl," full of gay sex and the forbidden words: cunt, cock, shit, and fuck.

"At his trial, Lawrence and the new literary world were lucky when the conservative Judge Horn decided: *'An author should be real in treating his subjects and be allowed to express his thoughts and ideas in his own words.'* Judge Horn also reaffirmed the decision in Roth v. the United States, in which the Supreme Court set forth the legal doctrine that a work must be totally lacking in social importance to be deemed obscene. Lawrence was largely responsible for Allen Ginsberg's financial independence. Allen was one of the few poets able to live off the sale of his work. As Ginsberg's publisher, Lawrence was generous with royalties. But that didn't stop Ginsberg from snubbing Lawrence when he flew from San Francisco to New York to read his own poems. After the reading, Lawrence flew to Chicago, and when I saw him I noticed his sadness. After some questioning he revealed that Allen had neither attended his reading, nor phoned, nor sent a card to let him know why.

Because of Lawrence, the word got around and we began to receive manuscripts, including some we soon published, from Jack Kerouac, Ginsberg, and Burroughs. When Irving Rosenthal called me to visit him and discuss what Burroughs had sent is one of those indelible moments reverberating through my memory.

"You see, Irving Rosenthal, the editor of the *Chicago Review*, was short, dark, and Jewish. While I, Paul Carroll, the magazine's 'guest poetry editor,' was tall, fair and Roman Catholic. Irving was a gay psychology student. I was a straight poet, extensively published in the *Chicago Review*, and teaching at Loyola University. But though we may have seemed to be opposite types, we were actually working together, trying to develop new forms of literature that found no outlet in the world of little magazines. We were looking for writing 'with more adventure, guts, even gaudiness.'

"What are we going to do with these pages, Paul? We are in Irving Rosenthal's stark white apartment, a single peacock feather on the wall. His plaintive question is about a messy heap of onionskin papers in a box on his desk.

"'Blast it if I know, Irving,' I said, fingering some of the many pages sent to us from California by Allen Ginsberg. Many were crumpled, smeared with ink and Moroccan food with scribbled notations in the margins – any editor's nightmare.

"'Irving, read a page; pick any page from the box,' I say.

"'Let's try this one,' Irving says, holding aloft a page as if it were a revolutionary banner.

"He reads:

Your reporter bang thirty grains of M a day
and sit eight hours inscrutable as a turd.
"What are you thinking?" says, squirming,
the American Tourist. 'To which I reply,
"Morphine have depressed my hypothalamus,
seat of libido and emotion, and since the front
brain acts at second hand with back brain
titillation, being a vicarious type citizen can
only get his kicks from behind, I must report

virtual absence of cerebral event. I am aware of your presence, but since it has for me no affective connotation, my affect having been disconnect by the junk man for the non-payment. I am not innarested in your doings. Come, shit or fuck yourself with a rasp or an asp – 'tis well done and fitting for a queen – but the dead and the junkie don't care" They are inscrutable.'"

"'Good grief,'" Irving says. 'Who is this guy?'

"'Well, Irving, I wrote to him in Tangiers and he answered without punctuation: *'Name Wm Seward Burroughs III Sole male heir of Burroughs Machine Corp St Louis Mo Harvard Phi Beta Kappa 37 with postgraduate work in anthropology and psychology Columbia For the past 15 yrs have been drug addict I am homosexual Who are you???'*

"'Well' I say, "'we are magazine editors hunting for new exciting writing, aren't we? Let's make a list of the problems we might have with this manuscript after we both have time to examine it thoroughly."

"Oh Paul, I'm certain it was exciting for you and Irving, courageously considering this new writing. But did you sometimes think you were in cuckoo-land, when working with Burroughs and Ginsberg? They were so different from your experience. At least you have never told me you were involved with theft, murder or drugs."

"Honey, they were unique rebels, not cuckoo, at least, not compared to my mother. You remember how I told you when I came home and told her I had been made captain of my high school football team she said: "You always had such beautiful ankles, Paul.""

"Dear, you look exhausted and that last memory didn't lift your spirits. Let's call it an evening."

"You're right. I am bushed. But now that I have started on the road to *Big Table* I damn well want to finish it. It just won't be tonight. Help me, dear, we are both exhausted and may need to pool our energy just to get to bed. Even the sky is tired. Look outside the window; there's neither moon nor stars in sight."

Irving Rosenthal

The next evening Paul said, "Let's go outside tonight. I know it's crisp weather but I want to smoke my cigarette stub without filling your lungs with more damn smoke. Also, I like to see Kayo chase his black tail around and around."

"I'll bring the usual wine and snacks," I said, looking at the threatening sky. Paul was contentedly puffing on his cigarette stub, leaning his head toward the creek to catch its music.

"Honey, I'm having another lucid memory about what happened fifty years ago. It's like a freight train barreling along through my mind."

"I've heard your memory records before, Paul. They remind me of an old television program – *You Are There.*" Sitting between the Chinese chestnut trees, a plaid blanket covering his lap, Paul sips his wine, winks at me and starts to speak like one of those holy men from India, Rajasthan men who can entertain villagers with tales from the Upanishads from memory, dusk to dawn.

"The following week, Irving and I were slogging through light snow to meet in the office of the *Chicago*

Review and compare notes on the merits of publishing what Kerouac has named *Naked Lunch.*

"'Obviously, Irving,' I say, 'our foremost question is, will we go to trial for printing obscenities? Burroughs's writing is consistently peppered with every known four-letter profanity. It's the work of a writer who is homosexual and a drug addict. Irving, we both know that the San Francisco city police arrested Lawrence Ferlinghetti for publishing Ginsberg's poem "Howl." I just read it and I believe we can draw comparisons between that poem and *Naked Lunch,* don't you? While Lawrence won the court trial on the basis of overall redeeming literary merit, how do we know what a different judge, here in Chicago, will rule?'

"'I agree, Paul, but since the *Chicago Review* is a university publication we can count on their legal counsel to represent us in court.'

"'Well,' I say, 'no one has complained about the Ferlinghetti poem we published this winter, *Pictures of the Gone World.'*

"'Yes,' Irving says, 'but there isn't a single four-letter word in the poem. The only shock is: *It was a face which darkness could kill / in an instant.* It wasn't the typical what you, Paul, call "gray-flannel poetry" printed in the *Chicago Review* before our editorship. We are moving, as steadily as possible, away from the usual academic poetry, found, for instance, in *Poetry* magazine.'

"'And,' I ask, 'what about *Sewanee Review, Partisan Review, Hudson Review*? Are their selections daring, gutsy? We both know the answer, Irving. What little magazine is publishing writing by a drug addict – *Evergreen Review*?'

"'Well,' Irving says, 'they printed "Howl" but deleted what might have been offensive.'

"'Irving, let's momentarily forget about the censorship dilemma. This is my main question: Is this work comic? I believe it is – absolutely funny and unique! I don't know of any other writing like this. I think we have to publish it, don't you? Or, in the future, look back and reckon we were cowards.'

"'Paul, we've worked together for a while. You know me well enough by now to realize how strongly, as a homosexual, I want to publish this writing. Allen Ginsberg is one of the few authors we know who is out of the closet.

I want to do everything I can to crack this impasse in our society – the discrimination against anyone seen to be different. But to print this with a minimum of repercussions we have to have a strategy.'

"'Oh, I agree,' I tell him. 'So tell me what you're thinking?'

"'My idea,' Irving says, 'is that rather than presenting these vignettes in their entirety we need to print a sampling, a small excerpt. We've already decided to print Jack Kerouac's ideas on poetry in the spring 1958 issue. An excerpt from *Naked Lunch* could fit into the same San Francisco issue along with Ginsberg, Kerouac, and Robert Duncan.'

"'You mean, run it up the flagpole and see if anyone salutes.'

"'More like let's print a bit of it and see if anyone throws tomatoes at us.'

"'Well, yours is the only tactic on the table, and, Irving, you now are the only one who can edit this perverse Burroughs manuscript. You and I know it portrays life as a nightmare where everyone is addicted to drugs, power, or sex.'

"'I know, I know, Paul,' Irving says. 'It's a mess of words. Editing it will be a labor of love fueled by a lot of coffee.'

"Irving and I had no idea that the San Francisco issue and the one to follow in the summer, focused on Zen Buddhism, were to be the best-selling issues of the *Chicago Review*. We also didn't know who would throw the tomatoes."

A slight drizzle filtered through the chestnut leaves and started to dampen Paul's memories as well as dilute our wine.

"Rain. I guess it proves once again that we have no control of the weather, Posie. But then I will always be grateful to the rain in Bloomington for pushing me into the library where I met Joyce's *Ulysses*. So I can't complain. Would you give me that tray to cover my head while we go inside?"

Censorship Begins

Last evening's rain continues, not as drizzle but as a steady, tin-roof-pounding symphony. I shake off my raincoat in the springhouse before entering our old kitchen. Its cabinets are layered with at least forty years of white paint, some of it speckling the glass-handle knobs.

Walking across the squeaky oak floor to Paul's study, I ask, "Well, Paul, who did throw the tomatoes?"

"The first one was lobbed by a local reporter, then the university pitched in. Have a seat and I'll share it with you, dear.

"It was autumn, a lovely time on the University of Chicago campus, or anywhere in the Northern Hemisphere, for that matter. I remember looking out the window at the leaves, in their startling colors, pomegranate red, pumpkin orange, lemon, start their inevitable pirouette down to the ground.

"Irving entered the *Chicago Review* office with his mouth dragging down to his soles.

"'Lad,' I said, 'what's bugging you? We should be the happiest editors on this planet. Your strategy for slowly introducing *Naked Lunch* to our readers has worked. We have no complaints, and the spring [San Francisco] and summer [Zen] issues are the best-selling in the magazine's history. We have tripled our sales! I am sorry you had to fire two associates who didn't appreciate our taste for Burroughs. But I still think the reactions to the magazine issues have been quite astounding in their welcoming reception.'

"'A big ripe tomato just smacked me right in the face,' says Irving. He asked if I had seen that day's *Chicago Daily News.* Right on the front cover – the *front cover* -- was a story titled 'Filthy Writing on the Midway.' Columnist Jack Mabley blamed the university for allowing us to print our various writers, all of whom he lumped together into the Beat category. He called us immature and irresponsible editors and writes this about our authors: *The obscenity is put into their writing to attract attention.*

"'I told Irving not to blow a gasket. Another author once told me that any press is good press, critical or not. He said count the column inches to gauge how helpful the article will be. It's especially important to have a photo. I asked Irving, 'Did the *News* article have a photo?'

"'No,' Irving said. 'No photo.' But he wondered

how the university was going to respond. He reminded me that the *Chicago Review* was already a minor annoyance in their eyes, ever since a previous editor ran up a $7,400 bill for a print overrun that they had to pay.

"'I wish Robert Maynard Hutchins was still the chancellor,' I said. 'There never was a question about his integrity and, HELL – with a few words he was able to convert Mr. Walgreen, the drugstore magnate, who was hunting, like Joe McCarthy, for communists among the faculty. Walgreen ended up being a weekly lunch chum of Hutchins and contributed half a million to the university.'

"'Chancellor Lawrence Kimpton is no Hutchins,' Irving said. He remembered when I told him how Hutchins denied a trustee's offer of a million if he would just reinstate football on campus. All both of us could do was wait and see what happened. Kimpton was afraid of how the trustees would take the news.

"It was barely a month before Irving resigned as editor and left the University of Chicago. Following Allen Ginsberg's advice, Irving also left Chicago to settle in New York City. The next day all the rest of us, save one editor, followed his lead and quit the *Chicago Review*.

Suddenly a recently enlivened little magazine had basically closed its doors. How could this happen in America on the basis of one newspaper story?

"I wrote to Irving: Why can't they ever grow up and dig that Burroughs is talking about us & them & the truth of wot they really go thru but are so spooked & full of the habit of lying that they can't see with their own two eyes?"

"But, Paul, why did you all leave?" I ask.

"Because the university forbade printing the winter issue. It was to have published 'The Garment of Ra' and 'Further Sorrows of Priapus' by Edward Dahlberg. It also was to have more selections from Burroughs's *Naked Lunch.* We couldn't stay when they wanted us to be their puppets."

"The university caved in to one single angry columnist? I don't think that would happen today. Paul, tell me what you think was different in the fifties as an era, different to life as we experience it today? Remember, I was in grammar school during those years."

"Posie, it was Adlai Stevenson who said that fear was a major motivator in America during the fifties. It was fear that started the massive construction of a nationwide network of new highways whose purpose was to provide mass evacuation in the event of a nuclear attack, as well as landing strips for planes. It was also fear that prompted school bombing drills shoving students like you to hide underneath their desks for protection. We knew we had dropped atomic bombs so we thought another country– probably Russia – might well do the same. It was fear of a communist takeover that prompted government officials to cooperate with Senator Joseph McCarthy in his witch hunts and blacklisting of supposed communist conspirators. Everybody was fearful: the feds, the cops, schools, even media. Lots of groups that would defend free expression today. In our case, publication suppression, Chancellor Kimpton feared future university donations might dwindle as a result of bad publicity from the *Daily News* editorial.

"Irving wrote an editorial in the first *Big Table* issue, which stated: *I was told that the magazine had a chance to survive if the coming Winter Issue were 'toned down,' but Mr. Wilt [Napier Wilt, faculty advisor to the Chicago Review] was unable to tell me exactly what 'toning down' the Chancellor had in mind. At this time I think Mr. Wilt and I assumed that at worst I would have to substitute asterisks for any four-letter words.*

"A few days later – *I learned on one day that I absolutely could not publish Kerouac or Burroughs in the Winter Issue. On the next day Mr. Wilt...said that the Winter Issue must be completely innocuous'. ... On November 17... I told him that I could not edit a magazine under the conditions he gave me.* On November 18, six of the seven staff members who held the rank of editor resigned"

"How did you feel about resigning, Paul?"

"Posie, it was one of the most unique moments of my life! Irving and I had poured our hearts into a magazine issue, our baby, and we were now told we couldn't publish. Chancellor Kimpton and the two faculty advisors of the *Review*, English teacher Richard G. Stern and art historian Joshua Taylor, claimed they were removing our independent editorship because we lacked the catholicity of literary judgment. I replied that their charge was both inaccurate and oddly parochial. It was like being murdered while you sleep. All the writers who thought their work was going to be published had to be notified. Their work for the *Chicago Review* was in limbo. Then the feeling of betrayal by an institution I loved and which I thought should act with integrity was stabbing me in the back.

"I was distressed over Professor Wilt's actions. He had been my advisor. I can still remember my senior year, when I was in Fulton Hall on the University of Chicago campus, knocking on his door.

"He called out for me to enter. Here was Wilting on his sofa, a rotund, friendly figure dressed as always in trousers held up by both a belt and suspenders. Cigar odor perfumed the air almost masking a faint musty scent from hundreds of books in shelves along one wall.

"He motioned for me to sit down, then asked whether I trusted Lockridge's narration.

"Of course, I understand he's referring to the narrator of events in, the novel we had discussed the previous week.

"'No sir,' I told him, 'I have always felt that Lockridge seems pretty uptight. An asshole.'

"'Yes. I've never liked the man,' he replied.

"What I loved about those dialogues with the good professor was that he always referred to fictional characters as individuals who are alive, breathing in our time and space. Belonging not to the nineteenth century, but to all times. They are not black ink on a white page; they live eternally in our minds and collective knowledge. We can talk about them almost as members of our extended family. I was embarrassed that Professor Wilt had not acted more nobly.

"Because of the censorship we all decided our issue could not end this way. We had to publish it, somehow, ourselves.

"Because of this censorship we gave birth to a new magazine, *Big Table*, whose first edition would contain exactly the material suppressed at the University of Chicago. All the publicity about the university suppression and censorship, that had trickled out from the campus to local newspapers and then to little magazines across the country was solid gold, predicting certifiable success for the new magazine. After all, the censorship of Allen Ginsberg's "Howl" in San Francisco in 1957 had made him a well-known author. Eventually *Howl and Other Poems* sold a million copies."

"But, Paul, where would the money for publishing

come from?"

"That, Posie, was the rub! Where would the money come from? Censorship is like hushing a child, with a hand over its mouth to keep it quiet, but in stopping the child's breath, it never speaks again. We wanted our child to speak! But how?"

"Enough, Paul, it's time to quit speaking, at least for this evening. You've talked too much and your voice is fading."

"Yes, *mon capitain*, you're right, dear. To bed we go. At least we can snuggle."

John A. Carroll

The angels must have made the day just for us. Seated in the shade of the chestnut trees we are enjoying the evening breeze and the sounds of Beaver Dam Creek. Nearby there is a large willow tree whose branches drape the ground. A breeze catches and sways them the way a horse tosses its mane. In a few seconds the breeze stirs the other side of the tree, and the giant horse shakes its tail.

Setting the picnic table with wine, goblets, and snacks, I thought, oh please, make this moment last forever for us. If only time would freeze, come to a complete stop.

Paul puts in my lap childhood photos from the family farm near Chicago. Here, he shows me, is his dad, John A. Carroll, with round face, blond hair, quietly handsome, sitting in a wicker rocker with Sam, their white Samoyed, at his side. There is Paul on his lap, a two-year-old, blond and round-faced like his father.

Paul told me, "If I ever acted courageously, standing up for what I believed in, both in the case of censorship with the University of Chicago and the U.S. Post Office, I know my father was my example. When the controversy was all over this is what I wrote: Having to fight for Big

Table is good. Concrete things like this seem to ram home to me that certain things like this are valuable, worth a fight and not just fancy talk in a classroom.

"I've told you my Dad was a titan, a self-made millionaire in the nineteen twenties and thirties. He made his fortune in banking and real estate."

"You've told me before about your father's banks and the Flossmoor subdivision. I just wish I had met him. Nineteen forty-four was both the year I was born and the year your dad died."

"Banks and real estate were only part of his empire. His real wealth lay in his ability to dream and make those dreams happen. The Hyde Park National Bank, for example, was the main bank in its south-side Chicago neighborhood. It opened in 1929, ten stories high, stone clad, designed by a German architect. The bas-relief sculpture over the entrance depicted two boys, my brother and myself, with Dad. We were the sculptor's models.

"I vividly remember one of the directors, a Mr. Tom Collins. I was only a boy when I heard his story at the dinner table. Tom had appeared drunk at one board meeting. My father blew his top and ordered him out, yelling, 'You're drunk, Tom! Go back to County Clare.'

"At the start of the next meeting Old Tom was sitting like a mouse in a corner of the huge room. Slowly he worked his chair forward until he was back in the thick of planning, saying, 'Now, John A. I was down by Grand Crossing Park.' While he didn't admit anything, the other directors knew he was chatting it up in the local bars. He continued, 'Ah, you know they have no bank there; they're keeping their money in the church. I believe we should be putting a bank down there. T'would be good business.'

"Well, Old Tom Collins was generally right three out of five times, and that was worth millions.

"Then, when the Depression came, my father traveled to Washington to testify on behalf of neighborhood banks. But it was to no avail; federal bailout money all went to the downtown banks. In 1933 they foreclosed on Hyde Park National. Federal receivership laws required only fourteen cents on the dollar to be reimbursed to a depositor. Between then and 1942 my father liquidated about six million dollars of his own money to guarantee that seventy cents on the dollar was paid out instead. He told me he knew his depositors, and he would not be able to look them in the eye if, like Scrooge, he kept his money for himself. Later on I became acquainted with some sons of bankers who tucked all their money in home vaults. These were nice enough men, but weak. I wouldn't rely on them to save us in hard times."

"I'm glad your dad truly cared for his bank depositors. They were people to him, not just numbers. I've never heard of any banker acting so generously with his own money. At least not the bankers we have today. I admire him.

"Paul, let's change places. Let me read part of your poem before it gets too dark."

I begin to read "Father."

FATHER

How sick

I get of your ghost.

And of always looking at this tintype on my desk

of you as a cocky kid:

Kilkenny's coast, rocks and suncracked turf

giving the resilience to your countenance

as you try to seem so nonchalant, posing

in a rented Sunday morning suit

spats and bowler hat:

a greenhorn off the boat.   And yet,

something in that twist of fist,
knuckles taut about the cane knob, shows
how you already seem to know
you'll transform that old cow-pasture of Hyde Park
into your own oyster.
The way you did....

"I can almost see your Dad in this poem," I say. But you've managed to stray from the subject of *Big Table*."

"I was hoping you wouldn't notice."

"Last night you were telling me how one editorial in a local paper had been the catapult for almost all the resignations of the editors at the *Chicago Review*. This morning, searching through the bookcase, I happened on the 1988 spring/summer issue of *Chicago History* where Russell Lewis, the editor, states that Gerald Brennan's article, '*Big Table*,' sets the tone for the coming decade, the culture of the avant-garde in Chicago. The magazine continued with articles about Martin Luther King Jr.'s 1966 marches in Chicago, Hull House's avant-garde theater, the 1968 Chicago Democratic Convention. Do you remember, included in *Chicago History*, is a vinyl recording of Ginsberg's reading of 'Howl' at the *Big Table* benefit reading, on January 29, 1959?"

"It has been a while since I've seen that magazine, but Jerry was right to say that our publishing attempts were fought by the university, the federal government, the media – groups you'd think should have been committed to free speech."

"Paul, has there ever been another censorship case that began at a university, and then was censored by the Post Office? I know you really love the University of Chicago. It was so obvious on those times we rode our bikes from the Near North Side to Hyde Park, cycling around the campus, bumping into writers like Norman Maclean. Paul, it must have been difficult to take up arms against the institution you love?"

"Yes, Posie, I love the university and Professor Maclean was one of my best teachers. I even liked the movie Robert Redford made from his novel, *"A River Runs Through It."*

"I remember my favorite time there was a dramatic Court Theater performance of *The Tempest*. Even the evening thunder seemed to be acting on cue as part of the play's cast. It was crashing and banging at just the right moments. Miraculously, rain never appeared, and we didn't have to scurry inside. But I'm pushing you ahead of your story. You and Irving, and editors Helen Shlien, Doris Nieder, Roland Pitschel, all wanted to publish the censored work."

"At some point we decided our issue could not end this way. We had to publish it, somehow, ourselves."

"But, Paul, where would the money for publishing have come from? Oh, Paul, I'm sorry for that question. I think you have to quit speaking, at least for this evening. You have talked too much and your voice is cracking. It's getting too dark out here, dear. Let's leave the creek music for the night creatures and go back to the house."

He nodded his head as he reached for my hand.

"Yes, *mon capitain*, you're right. To bed we go. At least we can hug."

Big Table Begins

This was probably the one time in history when poetry dominated the front pages of a major American city for nearly a week....The week marked Ginsberg's entrance onto a national stage, and it was a tremendous embarrassment to the University of Chicago.

Gerald E. Brennan, *"Big Table,"* Chicago History:
The Magazine of the Chicago Historical Society,
17, Nos. 1 and 2 (Spring/Summer 1988).

Early the next evening, Paul wonders just how the process of leaf coloring proceeds. It's happening right now all over the mountains. Why do gold and red arrive first while the ochers and browns are last? More importantly he wonders what's Posie cooking for dinner tonight. Nothing could be worse than steak soup; although he knows she is doing her best to make him comfortable with sympathy and affection. Having no teeth has whittled his eating choices down to slim pickings and he doesn't mean the actor.

"Look, Paul! Look at Kayo," I shout, walking out the door with a bottle of wine. Turning in his chair and looking out the window Paul sees our husky pup running in circles, chasing his own tail. It's a whirl of black and brown on the lawn. For a bit of dog food and attention

Kayo injects considerable mirth into our yearlong vigil.

"C'mon boy, here's a treat," Paul says as he walks outside. "I'm so glad coyotes haven't made a snack of you." "Sorry, Paul, I think it's too cold to sit by the creek tonight. Suddenly I find I'm chilled. Let's sip our wine inside."

"Fine with me; besides, something smells good in the kitchen."

"It's the pot roast in the slow cooker, Paul."

"Great. I always like pot roast, dear. Thank God you're the cook. I told you that Granny called me an ox in the kitchen."

"I remember you said she went to town to see a film on Vienna waltzes, mistakenly went to the wrong theater, and watched two National Geographic episodes of *Naked Women of All Nations* while you were home cooking the roast."

"That's right. I was studying for exams and forgot to turn on the oven."

"I wonder which bothered her more, missing Vienna waltzes or coming home to a cold roast?"

"Dear Granny, she kept our family together,

cooking, running the house, advising my dad. But let's get back to my story about the *Chicago Review*."

"I thought you and Irving were done, you had both quit protesting the university's censorship."

"Yes, we had, and we decided to start our own magazine, free from academic interference. Believe me, it wasn't an easy choice. Suddenly the university wouldn't be paying the bills, we would. None of us had a trust fund, just enough money to live on, day by day. We would have to raise a lot, probably over a thousand dollars, and none of us had experience in fund-raising."

"Well, it seems to me that you and Irving were totally committed to this idea."

"To tell the truth, honey, Irving and the other editors all knew I was the money man. We wanted to see this magazine get off the ground, but Irving was tongue-tied when it came to wooing possible donors. He just couldn't talk with them. I had the connections, and because of my experience with wealth, I was the only one comfortable dealing with a moneyed world.

"One advantage we had from the beginning was that the student government at the University of Chicago had reported the news of the suppression in their paper. Soon that news spread to local papers and little magazines across the country. It spread like wildfire, just the right subject to catch the attention of readers. No one could believe the University of Chicago would censor its student magazine. People from coast to coast were buzzing with the news, asking why the university shut down a successful magazine. Finding donors for our cause would allow us to pay for printers, the visiting writers' transportation, paper, stamps, and all the costs of a small publication emerging overnight. I solicited the owners of the Sherman House to lend their hall for a benefit reading and arranged for a radio interview of Allen Ginsberg, Gregory Corso, and Peter Orlovsky with talk show host Studs Terkel.

"All the publicity presented donor possibilities we needed. And now luck entered. Do you remember the evening classes I taught? My students were quite wealthy. They listened to me regarding literature. You can see how I dressed from these photos. (He hands me several publicity photos.) With three-piece tweeds, close-cropped hair, erect posture, I gave a general impression of confidence and wellbeing, even if I was almost broke."

"Paul, which professor offered you those evening classes while you were finishing your master's degree? Was it Napier Wilt?"

"Yes, though he was an important character involved with the university's suppression. He was the university negotiator who had to tell us the *Chicago Review* could not publish our new writers. I remember what an influence he was on me during my college years. If only he had acted more nobly during the negotiations between Chancellor Kimpton and us. I suppose he was afraid of losing his teaching pension.

"My evening students and I had chosen Joyce's *Ulysses* to study. People like Muriel Kallis Newman and her husband, Albert, were among my students. She later became a trustee at the Metropolitan Museum and, bless her heart, was one of the first to both give and loan me money. We scheduled benefit poetry readings. Almost a thousand people attended the best one on January 29, 1959, at the Sherman House. Allen Ginsberg, Gregory Corso, and Peter Orlovsky came to Chicago to read their poems. I can't forget a minute of it. [I have paraphrased most of the following but have kept some exact quotes.]

"I answered Ginsberg's question about what he should wear at the party before the reading: Dungarees, formal monkey suit, English waistcoat, Brooks Brothers special, or just plain jockstrap and roller-skates: anything you want to wear/ and be/ and say is all that matters at this party next Wednesday: the last thing I want is to throw you and Gregory and Peter, as you said, 'into a den of silent & attentive & polite & cynical' snobs.

"I told Allen: the woman giving the party, Muriel, is absolutely first rate. She is an extremely good and old friend of de Kooning and Franz Klein and she also knew Pollock well. She became one of the main benefactors who contributed to the birth of this new journal.

"For the party, I escorted Allen, Gregory, and Peter to the Drake Hotel on North Michigan Avenue. The Newmans had an apartment with catch-your-breath views of Oak Street Beach and Lake Michigan. Actually Muriel and Albert Newman were unique. Not just wealthy and handsome, they were intelligent, inquisitive hosts and decent people. These three poets would not be in Chicago if Muriel and others, like Bill Hartmann, who brought Picasso's sculpture to the Civic Center, had not sponsored

Big Table. I liked Muriel and Albert, they helped to fill my evening class with their friends.

"I remember sipping my delicious Bookbinder's soup, sent up from the Cape Cod Room, then leaning back in my armchair, happy that my short assault on Allen Ginsberg hadn't been vicious.

"I didn't mind Allen sticking his tongue in my ear, asking 'Do you like boys or chicks?' I admired Allen when he wrote that something new was happening with American prosody. But I found it different communicating with him in person. I found I had a visceral response to Allen's aggressiveness. When I wrote to him suggesting a connection be made in *Big Table* with earlier European writers like Apollinaire, he wrote back, 'don't load your pages with unnecessary baggage. It's camp to get hung up on Apollinaire. I know plenty of American poets. Their new writing is waiting for publication.' When Allen tries to tell me, as we both stand holding whiskey glasses, how I should write my own poetry, he tells me to *let natural accidents produce a point*. I know he's never read any of my poetry and I explode, throwing my glass at him. Where does that hairy beast get the nerve to tell me how to write when he has never read my poetry! The glass smacks, breaking against a wall, missing both Allen and a Jackson Pollock painting.

"Everyone in the room turns to the abrupt sound of violence. Gregory is already tipsy and starts to giggle, while Peter Orlovsky protectively rushes toward Allen. Muriel quickly diffuses the tension by herding us all to the dinner table.

"Now seated next to Albert Newman, enjoying the terrific food and amiable chatter, I feel my anger slowly dissolve into the gray smoky cigarette haze lingering above the table

"Honey," Paul sighs, "how naïve I was back then, believing artists can be tolerant in their considerations of different styles. That is what I wanted the new magazine to be open and inviting, big enough for all poetic styles. As I said more than once, I'd publish a poem by J. Edgar Hoover, if he wrote a decent one."

"Was this the occasion when Allen called you 'a horse's ass'?"

"Never to my face. It was in a letter he wrote to Bill Burroughs when I wrote telling him that I was ending *Big*

Table. I'll tell you about it later."

"So Ginsberg denied your value as a poet even while you were trying to publish him and his friends at risk to yourself. Read me a poem from that time, Paul."

"Well, OK. Here's one that was published in 1958, the year before, in the *New Yorker*. And he hands me a clipping:

WINTER SCENE

(AFTER BRUEGEL)

A solitary crow
        Crisscrosses across
This ice-cold sky. On tufts of snow
        Others press
        Feathers against their breasts
And stiffly perch in the poplars. Below,

        The worn hounds pad behind
                The hunters who hunch
Into the noiseless, gnawing wind
        And slowly crunch
        Along as if they're blind—
The carcass of a fox and haunch

        Of frost-caked rabbit twitch,
                Slung across
The tallest hunter's back, a stitch
        Of pelts and grouse
        Around another. That batch
Of peasants there against the house

        Shucks and roasts what's left
                Of last fall's corn.
Snow levels all, like love or death:
        To keep bones warm,
        Even if only in a loft
Or near the livestock in some barn

        Down in that valley town,
                Is all that matters.
Around the pond in the town,
        A child clatters
        On cow-bone skates. Beyond,
A pair of jagged mountains batters

        And almost cracks the ice
                That locks the sky.
But must those lonely hunters, restless,
        Haunted by
        A blood-red sun, press
Beyond into another valley?

        Yet this austere, stiff ice
                (And trees and snow)
Has its own barbaric peace,
        And if that crow
        Can't caw and can but freeze,
The wind moans gently on the snow.
                —PAUL CARROLL

"Quite a poem, Paul. Did you see the painting, *Hunters in the Snow*, at the Kunsthistorisches Museum in Vienna?"

"Yes, dear, that's where it ambushed me."

"Well, Paul, your poem isn't the spontaneous madness of Allen's 'Howl.' Highly structured, it has a brilliant hardness like a diamond. While it's short I think it has the sensibility 'Howl' has – that of a complaint. Allen's references began with his months in the insane asylum. In Brueghel's case that year of the painting was the coldest winter they had experienced. Maybe *you* were responding to the hunter's defeat and cold with your own despair but finally, at the end, optimism (barbaric peace)?

"But, Paul, you look beat, as in exhausted. I think you have dredged up some sweet and some bitter memories. Shall we take a break and head to bed?"

"OK, Allen. No, I'm joking. You can order me about, Posie."

Paul's Memory of *Big Table*

"Look out the window, Paul! It's all white-haired trees and bushes up to the ridgeline. I've read of hoarfrost but never seen it before."

"Yes, and look over there," he says pointing right, "it's 'a saturated meadow,' all white." Meanwhile a cherry wood log was perfuming the house as it crackled in the woodstove.

"Please help me understand all this, Paul. The university censored the Burroughs and Kerouac issue. Then, you and the editors who quit the *Chicago Review* started a new magazine, and then the Post Office attempted to censor your new magazine. You, Irving Rosenthal, Eila Kokkinen, Doris Neider, Barbara Pitschel, Charles Horwitz, and Al Podell all quit the *Chicago Review* in November. By December you had decided to start an independent magazine, *Big Table*. The work to be published in this new magazine was the same writing that had been censored by the University of Chicago?"

"That's it, minus lots of details Gerald Brennan included in his *Big Table* article in the Chicago Historical Society magazine." He hands me the magazine with a photo of J.F.K. lecturing at a podium with his back turned to us. A television set in the foreground shows us his face. Pointing to a section Paul asks me to read.

After New Year's 1959, the ex-editors began working feverishly on Big Table. *Some were trying to sell ads in the magazine; others drummed up publicity. Paul Carroll and Al Podell (the business manager) were both writing accounts of the suppression for little magazines. Barbara Pitschel gave an interview to the* Nation, *and a friend of hers who worked for the Associated Press tried unsuccessfully to put a story on the wires.*

"That's the basic outline, honey. It's what I remember. Now that I had raised enough money to start publishing *Big Table*, our next potential stumbling block, before we printed our first issue, came once again from the university."

"But you'd left them."

"I know, I know, but they thought they owned the intellectual property, the same manuscripts they wouldn't allow us to publish. It's crazy, isn't it? There we were in my apartment, working like lunatics on our first issue when the word came that the university wanted us to return the Burroughs, Kerouac, and Dahlberg manuscripts. As we negotiated, the discussion with the university's representative almost descended to kindergarten bickering. The university was saying, 'Give them back' and we responded, 'No, they're ours.' It's so funny now as I look back on it, distanced from the extreme anxiety. *Big Table* won the day on a technicality. Irving had never sent (so he said) letters of acceptance to any of the writers for this issue intended for the *Chicago Review*. He claimed that the manuscripts were sent from the authors to him, not the university. When the University of Chicago began to recognize the bad publicity it was receiving over this issue, they dropped the idea of a lawsuit. Now we were free to publish Jack Kerouac's 'Old Angel Midnight,' Edward Dahlberg's 'The Garment of Ra,' and 'Further Sorrows of Priapus,' William S. Burroughs's *Naked Lunch*, and three poems by Gregory Corso. Issue number 1 of Big Table had a striped red, white, and blue cover and cost one dollar. I couldn't find a single printer in Chicago who would take on the work! We were exuberant when the issue came back from the Profile Press, in New York. Gathering in my apartment on Dearborn Street we opened bottles of champagne, dancing and twittering for hours.

"Just when we thought our problems were over, disaster struck by way of the U.S. Post Office. By chance we began to hear that they were not delivering copies of *Big Table*. Our advertisers, New Directions, Beacon Paperbacks, the Gate of Horn, and *Partisan Review* were asking for their copies. One large batch of 400 magazines had been delivered to the main Chicago Post Office. That office decided to investigate the written material while smaller mailings from other offices had been delivered.

"I was in the seventh grade when this happened, so forgive me if I don't understand. Why did they impound *Big Table*?"

"Gerald Brennan explained it in his article. Would you read from here," he said pointing a paragraph....

$1

BIG
TABLE 1

THE COMPLETE CONTENTS OF THE SUPPRESSED WINTER 1959 CHICAGO REVIEW

JACK KEROUAC

OLD ANGEL MIDNIGHT

EDWARD DAHLBERG

THE GARMENT OF RA

FURTHER SORROWS OF PRIAPUS

WILLIAM S. BURROUGHS

NAKED LUNCH

By the latter half of the 50s, the smut question was burning in America...and plenty of groups were making sure ordinary citizens didn't soil their minds with literary filth. The Customs Bureau saw to it that such material did not enter the United States; the Post Office made sure it wasn't sent through the mails.

"So the Post Office thought your magazine was obscene."

"That was the key issue. I read later that the Post Office made an average of thirty-four arrests each month between July 1966 and January 1967. Actually, I could go to jail, pay a fine, or both. I lost so many nights of sleep for two years, until the court case was settled. In addition, a repercussion of the controversy appearing in newspapers was that I lost my teaching position at Loyola University. Suddenly I had no income while I was trying to support a new magazine."

"Paul, my first question is why the Post Office would bother with these mailings, your magazine, in the first place?"

"Good question, Sherlock. To tell you the truth, both the staff and I suspected that someone, probably at the university, had tipped off the Post Office. It was a suspicion based on your question, why would the Post Office be interested. We had our suspects, but no conclusive proof. At the later trial the Post Office presented only one letter in its prosecution. I can well imagine some professor who was caught in a bind, knowing they were guilty of having worked against free speech, and they didn't want to see us succeed. At any rate, this was a serious problem. In the last issue, *Big Table 5*, I wrote:

> Big Table #1 *was originally banned in March 1959 and over 400 copies impounded by the Post Office. The Illinois DE staff counsel was appointed to the case. At the request of Big Table a Post Office administrative hearing occurred in June 1959 at the Main Post Office, Chicago. Among the distinguished men of letters and educators who testified either in person or by letter for the right of the people*

to receive Big Table #1 *through the mails were: Jacques Barzun, John Ciardi, Reverend Pierre Delattre, Lawrence Ferlinghetti, Allen Ginsberg, Hans W. Mattick, Norman Mailer, Hoke Norris, Harold Taylor, Lionel Trilling and Anthony C. West. Paul Carroll testified as the publisher of* Big Table. *The Post Office attorney, in turn, produced one letter denying the literary merit of* Big Table #1. *This was written by August Derleth of Sauk City, Wisconsin. The result of the hearing was that the Post Office declared* Big Table #1 *not fit to go through the mail.* Big Table *then filed suit in the United States District Court of Chicago charging that the postal ban was unconstitutional and that the issue was a legitimate literary effort."*

"Your Sherlock has two questions. Where was Jack Kerouac's name among the defense witnesses?"

"You're tough. Jack bowed out, sending us a postcard instead. In it he said he didn't care if he was published."

from: KEROUAC

> Dear Paul
>   Did you receive ms. of Visons of Bill for
> Big Table? Or reject it? If you've rejected it
> please send it back at once, this address.
>   Also, Laurence Ferlinghetti is still
> waiting for copyright on Old Angel Midnight so he
> can publish his City Lights edition of it, for which
> I've written 5000 additional words and did the cover
> design. What's the story on that copyright?
>   As a writer I have no time to fiddle with
> court decisions about publishability or no, I dont
> even care whether I'm published or not, and never did,
> and that's why (as Irving suggested) I couldnt go to
> Chi to appear——I wrote all these things never ex-
> pecting them to be publisht anyway ..it's just a cul-
> tural accident that it was or wont eventually *JacK.*

"Well, his response didn't help you any, did it? Also, as I look at *Big Table 1*, I only see Irving Rosenthal, editor, and Albert N. Podell, business manager, listed. What happened to the rest of the staff?"

"You are observant. I dropped my name from the masthead for fear I would lose my teaching position at Loyola University. As a Catholic institution they were rather conservative. For all the good it did me, they fired me anyway, for no specified reason and over the protests of my students. I had this sword hanging over my head, as a result first of the university and then the Post Office. I was editing new issues of *Big Table* at the same time I was searching for a new job."

"It must have been an excruciating time for you."

"Yes, but also exciting, especially with hindsight. Our ACLU attorney, Joel Sprayregen, came through like a trouper. I was chagrined that I had questioned his experience at the beginning of the trial. Looking back on it all, the fear of jail, fines, loss of jobs falls away and it's like seeing the fantastic hoarfrost tonight. Maybe we can both dream about it when we sleep?"

Editing *Big Table* Was Heaven

I slept fitfully last night but the thrashing of the wind and rain did not prepare me for today's sight of bare tree skeletons surrounded by sacrificial mounds of leaves. They reminded me of lines from Paul's poem "George's Gap":

> The wind on George's Gap today is like a boxer
>
> smashing the tall grass and the tree and me
>
> as if we were pieces on a chessboard

It's so hard to remember that it was only year ago that Paul was driving to George's Gap and parking his white Jeep off the road, at the top of the Gap. Sitting there, writing poetry, he had a commanding view of the ridge-tops and valleys stretching all the way down to the town of Boone. But he hadn't expected the neighborly nature of passersby. They would stop their cars, roll down their windows, and ask if he needed assistance. Irish in his genes, Paul would begin to gab with them and often concluded their visit by selling them a copy of *The Beaver Dam Road Poems.*

Settling in our chairs in Paul's study tonight I tell him again how much I love his dedication in that book. He opens the cover with its map of Beaver Dam Road to read:

TO MARYROSE / If you could you'd walk about on Mars / I like everything about you / my Biblical wife.

"Paul, I've always wondered what you meant when you called me Biblical. I'm certainly not a churchgoer?"

"Well, honey, you were the one who led us here, to this promised land. Partly that's what I meant. I will think about it. I wonder if cancer is affecting my memory. Suddenly I'm having trouble remembering details. Would you please get out my copy of *Chicago Tales*? You know it, that slim book on the second shelf down in the bookcase."

Bringing back a small book with a cover photo of John Alexander Carroll, Paul, and Sam, their Samoyed dog, I ask, "Didn't Herman Kogan's son, Rick, give you a marvelous review in the Chicago Tribune for this book and you sold out in Chicago?"

"Yes, see, you remember so well. Let me see what I wrote about *Big Table* at the time of this book, 1991, thirty-two years after the magazine ended."

Paul started to read, but in a few minutes stopped and looked up at me saying,

"You know now I remember this like I was the one

who lived it. I thought editing *Big Table* was heaven. I realized that literary scene was unique, fresh and explosive. As I and the other editors discussed what had happened we thought and had satisfaction in thinking the five issues we published, from 1959 to 1961, helped make that scene possible.

"We wanted *Big Table* to be a gathering place where new writers could publish and meet/read each other's writing." He reads a line from his *Chicago Tales*, 'Because we had to fight for the right to publish what we wanted when we wanted, *Big Table* also became one of the stations of the literary underground railroad of those years.'

"Some of the books, stories, poems we published later became *Naked Lunch* by William Burroughs, *City of the Night* by John Rechy, *Kaddish and Other Poems* by Allen Ginsberg, *The Branch Will Not Break*, James Wright, *Advertisements for Myself*, Norman Mailer, and *Because I Was Flesh* by Edward Dahlberg. I have immense satisfaction when it is remembered that this writing first appeared in an issue of *Big Table*.

"These were all such different writers and," he reads

again from his book, 'yet each of them shared it seemed to me then, and seems even more evident today, the love of candor, the expression of which was probably the single most important contribution made by writers of the late fifties and early sixties.'"

"Paul, because I am still learning about poetry, tell me how the work you published was different."

Nodding, he explains that earlier writing included intricate masks, like Yeats in "Ego Dominus Tuus" or Pound's persona created in "Homage to Sextus Propertius." The addict-narrator in *Naked Lunch* is William S. Burroughs; the man who admits in the poem "Lying in a Hammock at William Duffy's Farm on Pine Island, Minnesota" that "I have wasted my life" is James Wright.

"And," he says, "*Big Table* writers are exposing their own lives, including formerly taboo subjects; drug addiction, homosexuality, failure. The intense, narrow world of the homosexual whore and the johns and queens whom he attracts is depicted by Rechy again in fiction based on what is obviously firsthand experience. In the audacious miscellany of *Advertisements for Myself*, Mailer confesses the Faustian need to hammer himself into an existential hero who will explore anything, from sodomy to drugs to alcohol to endless ego trips. Dahlberg, however, retells the myth of the Sorrowful Mother and the Crucified One, implying that the tale is the only one that counts for anything in his 60 odd years.

"Similarly their language was as real as what we actually speak. Fussing over whether to say 'fuck' or 'f—k' or 'fug' was finally seen for what it had always been: some type of weird high from grammar school days.

"Honey, they were writing in a language really used by men as Wordsworth had asked for over a hundred years before. It was about time."

Turning again to me, he says, "I remember feeling we had moved out of a dusty attic full of cobwebs into the freshness of spring." He continues to explain, because I was in grammar school then, "The fifties had such fearful madness. Like hounding J. Robert Oppenheimer, who had dedicated himself in developing an atomic bomb for the United States. The FBI added him to its Custodial Detention Index so that in case of a national emergency he would be arrested. And of course, there were those insane witch hunts conducted by Senator Joseph McCarthy."

Chicago Tales

We have gone from fallen leaves to wondering when the first snow will arrive. Driving home from grocery shopping in Boone and turning from Bethel Road on to Beaver Dam Road I watch the light fog change its nature and become a slow sprinkle of snow. Close to home, a doe and her yearling run across the road from Stanley's pasture into the thick low growth and trees. I know there are tons of acorns in the woods. If deer, like turkeys, eat acorns, they have their dinner. For Paul and me it's a pizza I got in town.

As we settle down in his study he resumes his commentary on his book *Chicago Tales*. "You know," he says to me, "When I think about the *Big Table* days now, or when someone asks me what that scene was like, I am happy because all of the memories are good and I will have them all of my life. He reads from the book: 'It is fall of 1957, the year I became poetry editor of the *Chicago Review*. I am sitting in the basement apartment of the editor, Irving Rosenthal, tiny, bearded, always bundled in two or three sweatshirts, it seems, no matter what the weather, a doctoral candidate in the Committee on the

Human Development at the University of Chicago. My chair is surrounded by hundreds of typewritten pages that have been casually arranged by Burroughs in the large carton in which he's shipped them from Tangiers, Morocco. Soon, Irving will shape the manuscript into chapters and then suggest a sequence for the chapters themselves. As I read I can hardly believe our luck. Once the shock and surprise over the fact that Burroughs calls a cock a cock and admits in print to being both a junkie and a homosexual wears thin, the suspicion becomes stronger and stronger that this colossal, sprawling labyrinth of a manuscript with its raw, violent energy, its addictive and incisive humor stands a good chance of being a classic. It is called *Naked Lunch*.'"

Paul turns to me, "As I said, Irving became a good editor. He was the one who structured the pages into chapters and put the chapters into a sequence creating a book."

I ask him, "Was *Naked Lunch* Burroughs's title?"

"No, Jack Kerouac gave the title to Burroughs's writing as well as our new magazine. We received a telegram around the Christmas holidays of 1958. It came from Jack and he advised: 'Call it *Big Table*.' We had tried literary names like *Golden Fleece*, and place names like *Kenyon Review*. After endless lists we knew we were getting nowhere and wrote to Jack for help. *Big Table* is just what I wanted. Its bluntness and lack of pretension was Midwestern. It also indicated an open-house editorial policy. Kerouac said he got the idea when he looked at a note on his desk –'Get a bigger table.'"

"Paul, what happened to Kerouac?"

"Ah, sweetie, I always wondered what would have happened if Jack had followed Coach Leahy to Notre Dame and played football there instead of Columbia. Leahy asked him to come. Maybe he would have been saved, instead of bleeding to death from alcohol."

"What a shame. Speaking of alcohol, we're out of wine. It's late. I'm closing up this shop."

"I hear you."

Allen Ginsberg Is Reading

As I walk up to the barn, to put up the horses for the night, I look down at the dark imprints my boots leave in the white snow. But then I see "the girls" and they are snorting, bucking and looking toward the edge of their pasture. I know, from experience, there's a bear around. While it won't hurt them I still go back to the house for my rifle. Who would shoot a bear? Not me, but I can make enough noise to scare it off. So I fire toward the sky and start to sing loudly: "She'll be coming round the mountain when she comes…"

That's all I can do for the horses tonight, so back to the house, go to the kitchen, and pull out some hearty lentil soup to heat for dinner. It's not a meal at l'Escargot in Chicago, but it's filling. The sun is going down in a few minutes so Paul and I head for his study as I grab a new bottle of wine.

"Honey, I'm still reading *Chicago Tales*. This next section has my memory of poets reading for *Big Table*. Allen Ginsberg was the first, with Gregory Corso. It was quite emotional. Allen had tears in his eyes and a choked voice. He didn't have lots of hair then, he looked boyish while reading his new poem, 'Kaddish,' written on an unfolding roll of paper. It was a benefit reading for *Big Table* with more than 1,000 in attendance at the Sherman Hotel. Diminutive Gregory Corso read next, new poems 'Hair,' 'Marriage.' This event raised a lot of money for *Big Table*. My only sadness is that neither Allen nor Gregory thought to ask me to read, too.

"The Sherman House had given us their stage for free and so did Paul Sills, Bernie Sahlins, and Howard Alk, the owners of Second City. Monday nights, when there was no "Second City" performance, we had poets like W. S. Merwin, Kenneth Koch, Robert Creeley, John Logan, Robert Duncan, Paul Blackburn, and John Shultz read. All the money collected at the door went to the poets.

"I remember Lawrence Ferlinghetti reading for *Big Table* in the fall of 1959. It was a packed house and for the first time I saw bearded young men clutching Zen paperback books and wearing sandals. It was a new style.

"The crowd for Norman Mailer's reading was before a mostly middle-class audience at the Knickerbocker Hotel. Norman spelled out with wit and muscle the definition of 'hip' and 'square.'"

"Paul, I wish I had been at those readings. Although there were series we attended together: Poetry Center Readings, the Links Hall series, and then those that your students organized at bars and restaurants scattered around the city. How did you conduct *Big Table* business?"

"The editorial meetings, any meeting, took place in the one large room of my apartment at 1316 North Dearborn Parkway. When we weren't meeting or having a party I could eat and sleep and also provide a bed for visiting poets.

"Cartons of *Big Table* often reached the ceiling. Manuscripts to read and consider were spilling out of big wicker baskets. Our favorite fan letter came from Brooklyn, an unsigned ad for fertilizer.

"Our staff grows and then diminishes as graduate students join us and then move on. One of these is Jim Hoge, a graduate student in History, who at 32 will become the youngest editor in history of the *Chicago Sun-Times*. Helen Shlien, Doris Nieder and teenager Roland Pitschel are the permanent staff. Great people, each one of them!

"Remembering our meetings, I can see us still

drinking coffee, laughing and learning to trust our instincts when voting to accept a poem or story. Our editorial standards were simple: (1) There are no schools of writers. (2) Every poem, story or essay must be judged on its own merits alone, not by the author's identity, or what cause it might advance. 'If Richard M. Nixon were to submit a good sonnet, we would publish it,' I often said, and I meant it.

"Then there were the parties, with everyone jamming into my apartment, also *Big Table*'s office. Everyone was there: poets, Second City actors, my adult class students, ACLU attorneys, and book reviewers, drinking beer and talking ceaselessly. I wish I were at one of those parties right now.

"I can still remember when I decided to quit with *Big Table* 5 as the final issue. I was being ground into the pavement by constant work nights and weekends. I had no time to write my poems. I had just become an associate editor of *WFMT Perspective,* a forerunner to *Chicago Magazine,* and I knew I would have to spend a lot of energy on its publication. More importantly, most *Big Table* writers now had New York publishers and so it seemed as if the magazine had accomplished its job by helping make the work of new writers better known.

"But we achieved that goal without influence from university officials, advertisers, or foundations, because *Big Table* paid its own bills. Fridays at six p.m. brought relief from the worry that the printer would call to badger me about the money owed him. And even though the (7,500 to 10,000) issues almost always sold out, money was chronically short. Paying the bills ourselves gave us independence to publish those writers we considered excellent."

"Wow, Paul, you must be exhausted reliving all that."

"It was good for me. Thanks, Posie."

"Paul, they were good times for you, weren't they? There's one last detail I want to understand. Irving Rosenthal wrote at the end of his editorial in *Big Table 1*: A non-profit corporation [*Big Table Books*] has been formed...Paul Carroll will be its editor, and I can hardly wait to see his first issue for I have stolen number 1 from him to fulfill what I wish to be my last editorial responsibility.'

"So from that point on, *Big Table* was yours. But you were just as involved as Irving in putting out *Big Table 1*."

"Yes, I was. I just removed my name from the masthead in an effort to try and save my job at Loyola."

"And was it your lawyer, Marshall Maynard Holleb, who filed those incorporation papers for *Big Table*?"

"Yep, it was Marshall. You could always count on him."

"Don't I know it. If Marshall and his wife, Doris, hadn't intervened on our behalf with the Chicago Zoning Board, we would still be living in Chicago. With his important law firm, Holleb and Coff, all 300 lawyers, and Doris who was on the Chicago Planning Board; no creek music without their intervention."

"Well, Posie you know it's always dangerous to be the first, and we were the first to live in a warehouse in a preferred manufacturing zone. Of course the city didn't want us to sell our Ada Street property as a residence. They wanted the factories to stay."

"So, after three months of our desperate waiting, the city zoning board issued a letter that didn't set a precedent for residential sales, but allowed us to sell our property as a residence nevertheless. Chicago has always been the city that works, if you know the Hollebs."

"Well, up the Irish! Up us, the little guys."

Where'd You Get Your Grit?

"We can't go outside tonight, Paul. Leaves have fallen, there's a bitter wind, and the sky is black. Thank God for a bright crackling fire in the woodstove. Settling in the warmth of the dining room, we enjoy some soup and crackers and then relax in Paul's book-filled study. On the wall is a black-and-white photo by Aaron Siskind, showing two abstract figures made by gray paint sprayed on a black wall. It was a gift to Paul from Aaron whose series of photos The Joys and Terrors of Levitation was included in *Big Table 3*.

"Paul, you must have been frightened not knowing how to earn money to pay for rent, food, or the printer. Quite possibly other universities would blacklist you. We both knew of writers, musicians, actors who were hounded out of jobs by those bloody McCarthy men."

He nods his head, knowing Studs Terkel and Pete Seeger had been targeted. "It's a shame when your own government has it in for you. Even though I removed my name from the *Big Table 1* masthead, hoping to avoid trouble, I was fired anyway. One would hope, at a Catholic university like Loyola, that they would embrace honesty and say forthrightly, Paul Carroll, you are fired for being involved with a censored and controversial magazine. But that didn't happen. My teaching position was simply 'not renewed.'"

"But what prospects did you have at that time? I know the last resort, going to live with your mother, wasn't acceptable."

"It was my network of friends that saved me. I had known another University of Chicago student, Mike Nichols, who was in the theatrical world. He became the first radio announcer for a classical radio station, WFMT, founded and run by Rita and Bernie Jacobs. Mike had started a Saturday evening program called the *Midnight Special* featuring folk and jazz music. I ran into him at Jimmy's Woodlawn Tap in Hyde Park and while we discussed my problems he told me the station was looking for an editor. They wanted to start a magazine featuring their programming. What a blessing! His news might be my salvation."

"Didn't he do comedy routines with Elaine May? I seem to remember one in which he is a NASA engineer overseeing a Cape Canaveral launch, and Elaine calls as his 'only mother,' wanting to know why he hadn't called her on Mother's Day."

"That's them. Absolutely hilarious as she reduces him to a gibbering baby while in the background we hear the rocket countdown," Paul nodded, then took up the tale.

"So, the next day, I called WFMT and with Mike's introduction was able to get an interview with the station manager, Ray Nordstrand. With great hope and some trepidation I proceeded to LaSalle and Wacker Streets. Exiting the elevator at WFMT's floor I walked down a hallway filled with press photos of Pete Seeger and Mahalia Jackson, as well as Leopold Stokowski, Leonard Bernstein, and other famous conductors and musicians.

"As I entered Nordstrand's tastefully decorated outer office, I heard a Mozart piece playing. The quality of the station's programming had already made it a unique location on the radio dial. They refused to air canned advertisements; instead they required them to be read live by their announcers.

"In the reception area a middle-aged bespectacled secretary asked me to sit down to wait for the station manager. In a short time Ray Nordstrand came in: tall, dark, thin hair, black shoes with white socks. New York financiers would label him a Midwestern hick while Ray cleverly negotiates extremely good loan rates for the station. The tall Swede extended his hand and said, 'Thank you, Paul, for coming in this afternoon. Rita and Bernie discussed your experience and think you have all the requisite skills to tackle the job of editing our new magazine, the WFMT Perspective. We imagine the first issue will start with a few articles and the listing of our radio programming. Of course, there should also be a guide to Chicago cultural activities. My only worry is that your scandal with the Post Office may scare off our advertisers.'

'"Well, Ray,' I said, 'it hasn't hurt advertising for the next *Big Table* issues. In fact ads have increased. We're getting press in New York, and now London, as a cause célèbre.'"

'You may be right, Paul, but I need to discuss it further with Bernie and Rita. They were courageous enough to hire Studs Terkel when he was blacklisted and fired from his TV show. Your situation with controversy and governmental interference is not unlike his problems with the Communist hunters. I will let you know about the job definitely by tomorrow.'

"I stood up with a smile. 'Well, it was my pleasure to meet you, Ray, and I would enjoy working with you, and Bernie and Rita Jacobs. This station definitely has class.'

"As I left his office I was not quite sure whether my spirits were half-mast or lower. I felt something like the Delta satellite, which failed its launch that day and was destroyed. Back in the hallway I caught sight of a short man with a red-checkered shirt talking staccato style. As he suddenly waved at me I recognized Studs Terkel, resident genius and interviewer par excellence for WFMT. A tall, lean, muscled man wearing a blue shirt and blue jeans is with him. He matched the photo labeled Pete Seeger on the wall.

"'Hey kid,' Studs hissed. 'I suspect Ray waffled and didn't give you the job right out. I know the Jacobs's want to hire you. Bet on it! Ray is a great guy, but he is also a bean counter. Meet my friend Pete Seeger. He and I are going out for a drink. Why don't you join us as we walk across the river to Riccardo's? You two guys have some things in common. You need to talk.'

"Riccardo's was one of the more unusual bars in the Chicago area. Ric Riccardo, an artist, had opened the place and expanded it into two adjacent former speakeasies. It featured a padded leather bar shaped like an artist's palette. The walls featured a selection of paintings. Once we settled into an oversize booth, Pete got up, stretched his lanky frame, and moved toward one of the paintings on the wall.

"'Hey, boys, you have the hometown advantage,' Pete said. 'Come and tell me about this painting. It's obviously a portrait, but I'm not sure I would want to meet the subject. I don't think I've ever seen anything like it.'

"Studs, still the TV actor, begins a clever imitation of an Art Institute docent: 'This work is by the most famous Chicago painter, Ivan Albright. Have you seen *The Picture of Dorian Gray*? George Sanders, Donna Reed, Angela Lansbury, and Peter Lawford all act in it. Our Ivan did the painting for the movie, the repository of all Dorian Gray's sins.'

"I butted in on Studs's routine: 'It is realistic and then some. Ivan may spend over a year on a painting and when finally finished he will price it as high as a Rembrandt.'

"Pete said: 'I'll wager Ivan doesn't sell many paintings.'

"He doesn't need to,' Studs replied: 'Comes from a wealthy family.'

"I said, 'It's an obsessive painting, as though he had to capture on canvas every hair and capillary.'

"Now Studs asked: 'It makes you wonder what he was like as a father?'

"Our drinks arrived, so we exited the art tour.

'Studs,' I said, 'you mentioned that Pete and I had something in common, besides being tall and handsome, that is.'

"'Well, you both are being hounded by the dark shadow of our government and may have to go to jail.'

"'Studs, Paul and I are trying to forget that possibility. In my case, I was called before the House Un-American Activities Committee. They asked me about a quote in the *Daily Worker* which said I had performed at an Allerton Section housewarming and they wanted to know whether that was a section of the Communist Party."

I told them: "I refuse to answer that question, whether it was a quote from the New York Times or the Vegetarian Journal.'"

"'Did they laugh at your humor, Pete?'" Studs asked.

"'They kept hounding me with questions, as if I was their fox, until I told them: I feel that in my whole life I have never done anything of a conspiratorial nature and I resent very deeply the implication that being called before this committee implies guilt in some way. My opinions may be different from yours, or yours, Mr. Willis, or yours, Mr. Scherer, but I am no less of an American than anybody else. I love my country very deeply, sir.'

"'Well, there you have it, boys,' Studs declared, 'it's a sin to be considered different. I remember in my youth when grown men would stand on soapboxes in Bughouse Square across from the Newberry Library, to debate their opinions openly. They were exercising their First Amendment rights to free speech.'

"So I asked them, 'Is it different to think it's stupid to have children duck under their school desks to avoid nuclear attack? Or is it different to think that a waiter, whatever his color, should have a right to speak? And what if he's homosexual, or a woman? Is it different to think that they also have rights?'

"Well, boys,' said Pete, 'they socked me with contempt of court, and unless my appeal trial is successful I'm going to hope they'll let me bring my banjo with me when I march into jail.'

"'We live in a time of fear,' I said, 'afraid to consider the other. That is someone with a different political idea, a homosexual, a vagrant, someone not locked into a corporate job, home, and retirement.'

"'Now, Paul,' Pete asked after a slow sip of his root beer, 'tell me how did you manage to get within the firing range of our government? Are you printing blueprints for bombs or leaking secret government documents?'

"'No, I printed a magazine of some Beat writing. The Post Office thinks it contains obscene material. Pete, believe me, jail was not a destination on our agenda. We were just literary types working on a magazine, the *Chicago Review*, and hoping to find some lively writing. We had grown collectively bored with academic prose and poetry. We wanted something based on the life we experience all around us instead of Greek mythology or nineteenth-century stories. I heard from my pal in San Francisco, Lawrence Ferlinghetti, something new and lively was emerging. So we started to publish new work by Jack Kerouac, Allen Ginsberg, and William S. Burroughs. Unfortunately a local newsman, Jack Mabley, caught wind of our publication and wrote an article titled "Filthy Writing at the Midway." One thing led to another, and we editors resigned when we were forbidden to publish this new work. I was able to raise money to support an independent new magazine, *Big Table*, but someone tipped off the Post Office and they impounded most of our mailing. We're asking to bring this issue to trial. Potentially I could get five years in jail.'

"'Boy, they are tough here in Chicago! I only received a one-year sentence,' Pete said.

"'That's because songs live in the air and in our memory, whereas you can hit someone over the head with a magazine,' Studs suggested. 'Well you may both go to jail for taking a stand on what you think is right. Let's have a toast: To our conscience, may it always win out over our wallets.'

"'Hear! Hear!' Pete seconded. 'But I am surprised that a private university with such an outstanding reputation would keel over so fast just on the basis of one newspaper article.'

"Studs said, 'Both Paul and I went to the University of Chicago. Pete, we know that this is not the university's finest hour. I'll swear on my mother's grave that when I graduated from law school there half of my class went to work for the mob, even though we studied ethics.'

"Then Studs, the perpetual interviewer, posed a question: 'Well, you boys are like oak trees. Where do you think your grit came from?'

"'Well, I had a grandfather who was an abolitionist. He stood tall against slavery,' Pete responded. 'I think he threw some solid meat into my stew.'

"I answered with, 'And I had a father who liquidated most of his personal fortune to pay his bank depositors when his bank was stupidly foreclosed in 1933. He said he knew his depositors personally and could not cheat them the way the government allowed.'

"'My blessed mother,' Studs' hands were revolving like whirligigs as he spoke, 'had the foresight to withdraw all her money from the Reliance State Bank the day before the bank failed. She knew not to listen to the banker's reassurance. That was money she had earned through her hotel.'

"'Paul and Studs, here's a toast to our ancestors, brave men and women as well.'

"'Now that he can't hurt anyone else I'll give a toast to that mean spirit Joseph McCarthy, whose actions got me kicked off my TV show, *Studs's Place*. I can't wish any man ill, but I sure hope no one helps him come back from his grave. And I'll be cheering for Kennedy in the fall election. I already know that Nixon has it in for me. He was quoted with this happy tidbit, 'The Jews are just very aggressive and abrasive and obnoxious. The east coast newspapers which spotlighted the insanity of war on Cambodia and Vietnam were the work of Jews.'

"'Did I ever tell you boys how Mahalia Jackson once saved my hide?' Studs asked. 'I'd taken a job announcing for her radio show. At that time she was the Queen of the Air. These government men showed up at the studio waving papers they wanted me to sign naming people as communists. Mahalia looks over from her piano and asks me if it's what she thinks it is. I nod yes and she gets the show producer. She tells him simply, 'No Studs, No Mahalia.'

"'Those federal men were thrown off the set. Bless her heart!'

"Now our rebel trio was throwing conversational bits back and forth as though we were pitching poker chips into a high-stakes game where the pot was not winner take all but instead to share equally. As we bundled up our items and paid our checks, Studs said, 'Paul, you know those young poets you had read at the Sherman House for *Big Table*'s benefit, Corso and Ginsberg? Let me know when they're coming back to town. I'd like to interview them again.'

"As we walked out into the twilight, I said to Studs, 'Absolutely and Onward!' walking from those amazing friends with a spring in my walk."

"Paul, you're in such a good mood, remembering Studs and Pete."

"I may be dying but I feel great having been given the gift to meet and know some remarkable people. More money wouldn't help me right now, but these reminiscences do. They lift my spirits sky high."

"Well, I think we should move our spirits right into bed. Sweetie, changing the subject, did you hear from Luke?"

"Yes, he sent me a letter. You know how I always worry about my son. He's still living with his mother at age thirty, just like his old man. He seems to be all right, still playing his guitar with a band. But I do worry about his health and his future. Whether he's getting into drugs. It's so difficult not knowing.

"After I'm gone, Posie, I hope you will have enough money. I made a lot of it at times, mostly when I was married to Inara, [Luke's mother] but it disappeared, along with the Mercedes, the town house, and all that other stuff."

"I have this farm and a pension. I'll get by. Paul, have you finished your ciggie? The fire has died and it's turning cold. Let's go and warm up our bed."

Luke and Paul Carroll, 1974. Photograph by M. Phillips.

Posie's Memory of Allen Ginsberg

I heard a Ka-booom! that split the sky open and almost made me drop our wine. I quickly set down my tray as I called to Paul,

"Come quick. Look out the window! A frightful

storm is coming past Grandfather toward Roan Mountain."

"Wow! That looks like a witches' Sabbath! Posie! Start a fire in the woodstove. I don't think it will snow, but I bet it's going to chill our old bones."

Once we settled down with a sizzling fire and some wine, I asked Paul, "Have we finished with *Big Table*, I mean the magazine?"

"Maybe, but one aspect is missing. You met many of my poet friends almost twenty years after *Big Table* magazine. I'd like to hear once again your memories of them."

"You mean the mouse gets to speak?" I teased.

"You, a mouse? My god, what can you mean with your huge sculptures? More like a tiger."

"Well, tigers can also purr, dear. I'm delighted to share my memories, and I suppose I should lead off with Allen Ginsberg. I was with you those times when we attended his Chicago readings. I remember best the evening he came to visit us at Ada Street.

"Arriving alone, he was dressed like a professor in a blue suit, white shirt, and striped tie. His graying hair and beard were groomed. You later quipped you thought the change from his previous attire was preparation in case Stockholm called. I caught glimpses of you both in animated conversation on the sofa as you looked through a book Allen had brought while I was cooking and serving refreshments. The two of you were leaning toward each other absolutely absorbed in your conversation. While Allen's soft voice was calm, his hands constantly gestured in patterns close to his body. No longer the impassioned, rebellious youth, I thought: his dedication to Buddhism had led him to a gentler lifestyle. Most of all I remember when we walked with him down the spiral staircase to our warehouse front door. He gave us an inscribed copy of "Howl" and kissed me smack on my lips. He told us how he still lusted after a blonde 'Playboy bunny' type. Well I am neither blonde nor a playgirl, Paul."

"You're good-looking, dear."

"Well, thank you, but it was pretty cheeky to kiss me so brazenly right in front of you. Wasn't it in 1959 that he wrote you were 'a horse's ass'?"

"Yes," Paul replied, grinning "in a letter I didn't hear about till a year or so later. I had written Allen about the troubling financial woes and court trials *Big Table* was having and that I would have to close down the magazine with the fifth issue. He wrote in turn to Jack Kerouac who wanted permission for Lawrence Ferlinghetti to publish 'Old Angel Midnight' from *Big Table 1*. And while he told Jack I would probably say yes to the republication of Kerouac's prose poem, he also said, 'Carroll who's a horse's ass as far as that goes and a mild virago, but is working within his limitations as best he can and is not a total loss.' That's the only time in my life I have been called a virago. What fun! In one word he switched my gender as he insulted me. A MILD virago, no less.

"Allen didn't want *Big Table* to end. He knew it gave a convenient, daring outlet where he and his friends might have their work published. A total tyrant at times, he often tried to direct what should be included in my magazine. He would become enraged when I wouldn't publish more Orlovsky poems. Or Ray Bremser. He wrote Jack that I had always had an easy life and was ducking out when the going became tough, with no money, and the possibility of jail time. For my part, I couldn't count on being sent to a psychiatric ward, as Allen was when he was sentenced to jail."

"Honey, did you really think you might go to jail?"

"Hell yes! This was an arm of the federal government threatening me, and they had only recently sentenced Pete Seeger to a year in jail."

"Paul, it's obvious that you and Allen later made up as friends, after he called you names."

"Oh sure we did. We were young poets when he wrote that to Kerouac."

"How did you even know about his comment?"

"Ferlinghetti told me when he stopped in Chicago. He knew personally what it was like to go to trial on Allen's behalf and still be slighted by him."

"You included a poem of Allen's in your book of essays on individual poems, *The Poem In Its Skin*."

Paul hands over to me a hardback book with the dust jacket image of the rear of a man's head with short haircut and prominent ears, and a vague field in the distance, a photo by Aaron Siskind. Paul's essays are on individual poems by John Ashbery, Robert Creeley, James Dickey, Isabella Gardner, Allen Ginsberg, John Logan, W. S. Merwin, Frank O'Hara, W. D. Snodgrass, and James Wright. It had three printings from 1968 to 1970.

"Which of Allen's is your favorite poem, 'Wichita Vortex Sutra'?"

"No, 'Kaddish.' I wrote in the 1969 *Playboy* magazine interview I did of Allen, 'Allen Ginsberg's real accomplishments as a poet do not come from his public image or his political and social poems. The great Ginsberg poems are private. ("Howl," that labyrinth of personal sorrow is a very private poem.) The earlier ones were elegiac. In them Ginsberg mourned his own miseries and the insanity of his friend Carl Solomon, the death of his mother, the decay of his own body. The more recent poems are pentecostal. Tongues of fire flicker through them as Ginsberg wrestles with the Godhead the first American writer to do so since Melville.'

"I continued, 'for the first time in our poetry we have a poet who celebrates the ancient ritual invoking of the God. These poems are both invocation and confrontation. In them Ginsberg asks and gives no quarter. One must take them as literal, experienced visions, or not at all. What is hard to bear is the shock of seeing a modern American poet struggling like a Hebrew prophet with his God. The God whom Ginsberg invokes, hates, loves, mocks, copulates with, and weeps on his knees in front of, is terribly present....He is the barbarous, beautiful God who speaks from the Burning Bush.'"

"Allen wanted you to continue publishing *Big Table.* Did he influence you when you started publishing again?

"No, honey. It was almost as easy as licking my lips. Frank O'Hara's brother Phil was working in Chicago with the Follett Publishing Company, textbook publishers, and Phil wanted to be involved with something more creative. Frank told him to contact me and together we instituted *Big Table Books* as a division of Follett Publishing. I had incorporated the name Big Table in 1959. Suddenly I was editing again without having to pay the mortgage."

"Paul, I want to hear more about *Big Table Books,* but right now please continue with Allen. You know how maniacal I am."

"I know. That's how you finish your sculptures. All that welding and grinding. You just don't quit."

"I know I'm a fiend, but I really enjoyed rereading that *Playboy* interview you did with Ginsberg."

"Thank you, my dear virago."

"Reading it almost thirty years after its publication I

think Allen is more of a seer than Norman Mailer, whom you also interviewed in *Playboy* the year before."

"Tell me more, Posie, you've got my interest."

"In one respect, Allen was ahead of his time in espousing Buddhism. For me, the main champions of Buddhism in the fifties were Allen Watts, Jack Kerouac, Gary Snyder, and a Tibetan Buddhist community in New Jersey. And, of course, the wonderful exhibit of Tibetan life we'd visit in the seventies at the Field Museum in Chicago. Remember how we would go to the museum with Luke and the three of us would see a blue donkey stuffing a human victim down a well, a screen painting of Buddhist hell? In the sixties, American attention began to focus on the Buddhist monks in Vietnam who were practicing self-immolation. Think how things have changed, Paul. Today there are Buddhist retreats, monasteries all over America. We even have a practicing Buddhist priest in Blowing Rock. Tozan spent seven years studying in Japan."

"Maybe that's why I wrote that Allen was a mystic and could see ahead of his time. How else do you think he was a prophet?"

"I don't know if he was a prophet, but he seems to have had an alternative vision of our world, one not addicted to Wall Street. Also, I admire his candid courage in announcing he was queer. I've known women who made the mistake of unknowingly marrying homosexual men. What a disaster for them. His candor helped to crack the pervasive fear of coming out of the closet."

"Well, Posie, I wrote that my interview was 'a candid conversation with the hippie-guru poet laureate of the new left and the flower children.'"

"Did your interview with Allen for *Playboy* happen after the 1968 Democratic convention in Chicago?"

"Yes, honey, he was staying with me and my first wife, Inara. We spent almost eight hours talking together for the interview. I thought he had a conviction that only he and a few of his friends knew anything about the subjects he discussed. Here, read this part." Paul passes the magazine to me. I read: "The fame he's acquired since I met him in 1958 seems to have given him a little more assurance than he needs. But he's become a happier and merrier man. And he has a strong capacity to keep growing. But one thing that's never changed—and I doubt if it ever will—is that Ginsberg's a poet first and last."

"But Paul, I thought you didn't like his later poetry."

"That's true, but remember this interview was written in 1969. I also said this," and he points to the next segment and asks me to continue reading.

"'When he was in his late 20s and early 30s, he'd read his poems on stage, often bristling with anger, but with a compelling aura of intelligence and sweetness, wearing soiled blue jeans, a lumberjack shirt or black turtleneck and owlish Columbia University intellectual glasses. Clutching an endlessly unfolding scroll of poems, he would hunch forward, thrashing a simian arm, weeping, haranguing, caressing, as he built and built the long locomotive stanzas, his oddly boyish, grating New York voice hammering away until suddenly magically, something seemed to explode and the audience felt transported.

"Since he's become a guru and a world renowned poet, the gentleness and warmth that were once counterpoints to rage and indignation have begun to dominate his persona; candor, power and authority are still strongly evident: but for all his earthy profanity, I sensed about him, improbably enough, something of the holy man. Our conversation began with a discussion of his apparent evolution from Beat to beatific.

"'Allen: The world that opens up seems strange, familiar but forgotten: more real than the usual place because of deeper feeling, a doom significance, but at the same time, frightening. We forgot it's been there all along: it means we have been mad all along. So people out of shame and fear of exploring the future and fear of death—fear of life itself—close the doors and go back to their old Safety Habit, and call their own breakthrough a hallucination or freak-out abnormally.

"'I asked Allen, why?

"'Average young guys have been so heavily conditioned to living in the closed circle of night-club--money-machine-airplane-taxi-office-bank-roll-television family that they distrust other modes of consciousness and pathways of existence like knapsack-long-hair-far-commune-picket-line street-high-sign—that are viable and real. Here's the danger that the money man, thinking his security is dependent on money, afraid his supply will be cut off like junk from a junkie, may entirely reject his own unconscious, cutting himself off from his own nature and organic perceptions and becoming, as William Burroughs says, a "walking tape machine."

'"That's a precise definition of square, because a limited and therefore defensive social consciousness is set up which shuts out other life forms. It causes fear of strange experiences and suspicion of menace in black power and the yellow peril and flowery hippies and the purple virus from Venus -- conspiracies to invade our consciousness. Thus rises the whole social paranoia, personal in nature and individual in each man, which is known as the cold war. Now, if it were really safe to stay inside the shell of the white American image -- successful, protected, "viable," going up and down office buildings in carpeted elevators, it would be hard to get people out of that state of mind. But it's not even safe in that shell anymore. Limitations of perception imposed by such egotism are biologically and evolutionarily self-defeating. **I mean that our refusal to coexist with other life forms is causing a planetary ecological crisis.'**

"Well Paul, he was certainly right and prophetic with that 1968 statement, decades before we came to speak of depleted ozone layers and climate change."

"That is Allen's uniqueness. He is sui generis. And so are you, dear. You communicate with people, horses, dogs, and plants. Plants were part of Allen's extended family. He claimed he could see their spirits. It's like those ancient myths that once we could speak with animals."

"Or like the section in one of the Carlos Casteneda books where he and Don Juan are being pursued by a jaguar in the Sonoran Desert. Don Juan yells at Carlos to not think which way they are going, the jaguar can read their thoughts."

"Well, dear, can you read my thoughts?"

"Of course, you're tired and want to go to bed. Do you remember the morning we woke and found we had dreamed the same dream, but with subtle differences?"

"Yes, we dreamt of a soft summer where we floated up to trees abundantly full of so many types of fruit."

I move close to him, letting my fingers walk up his arm and then begin to kiss and nibble at his ear.

He sweetly takes my face in his hands to kiss me. When he stops he says: "Let's go and see what we dream tonight, sweetheart."

Judge Julius J. Hoffman

Tonight the moon is full, harvest-sized, a golden melon hanging above the ridgeline across Beaver Dam Road. Light breezes move past us, but it isn't cold. When I bring out the wine and glasses I see Paul slumped in a wicker chair. He lifts his head and turns to me.

"Honey, I woke this morning dreaming of my father's funeral. He passed away just months after you were born."

"I wish I had met him. Would he have said I had a mouth like a turkey's ass?"

"No, not you, dear. He said that when Uncle Ned brought home his intended for Dad's blessing. If you had seen Aunt Molly you would understand. My dad's judgment was crude, but not far off the mark.

"But just look at this business of my dying! My six - foot frame is shrinking, my skin knitting into a bag of wrinkles, my dear teeth now mere memories of old friends. I spend more time in the bathroom than at the dinner table, now with a new friend, ugly pink Pepto-Bismol. I'm a shell of my former self, and soon I'll leave behind taste, feelings, and thoughts accumulated for almost 70 years –

for what? I have collected mementoes, if not a fortune. There are books on shelves, awards, faded newspaper articles. What do these now mean and how important are they?"

A sudden backfire from an old truck traveling down moonlit Beaver Dam Road shakes Paul from his depression. He sits up straight, saying, "I just finished the poem I've been working on since last spring. Let me share it with you. See what you think. It's called "Bequest." "

This gentle, quiet early April rain tonight,

Its voice a ghost's

Against the windowpane. Outside,

The rain feels raw. Its chill the chill

Of lizard's blood; who wants to die? -- And yet, it's only fair

That others share

This peach of an earth, where we can think, and sing,

Make children, love, create,

Where we can walk among alfalfa and sweet clover tall

as rabbits' ears

And swim in arabesques like dolphins,

An earth where all of us are astronauts.

To the man or woman who 100 years from now

Occupies the space I knew –

I offer you this poem.

"Dear, those lines came straight from your heart generous and true."

"I'm so glad you like them. Do I get some wine now?"

"We are almost, almost done with *Big Table*, or at least the magazine. Later I'll tell you about *Big Table Books.*"

"Paul, I was looking at a copy of *Big Table* 5 and found your statement detailing the outcome of the Post Office hearing and your lawsuit against them. Do you remember it?"

"It was thirty-five years ago, but how could I forget? Would you like to read it for us?"

In my hands I had Paul's magazine, with an enchanting cover image of a long-haired beauty, her eyes closed, standing in a pond, a photograph by Harry Callahan of his wife, Eleanor, titled *Bather*. Inside was work by Douglas Woolf, Frank O'Hara, Edward Dahlberg, Frederick Tristan, Robert Duncan, Paul Bowles, Kenneth Koch, John Rechy, Bill Berkson, Pablo Neruda, John

Updike, John Ashbery, Harold Rosenberg, Davie Meltzer, Alain Robbe-Grillet, and John Shultze. After reading the long list of contributors I said to Paul, "No wonder Ginsberg called you 'a horse's ass,' he's not included."

Photograph by Harry Callahan, 1960.

I began to read aloud:

Big Table vs. Post Office

On July 5, 1960, Judge Julius J. Hoffman ruled from his chambers in United States District Court of Chicago that the Post Office Department ban on *Big Table 1* which charged that the issue was nonmailable because of "obscenity and filthy contents" – should be "vacated and set aside."

Big Table 1 was originally banned in March 1959 and over 400 copies impounded by the Post Office. The Illinois Division of the American Civil Liberties Union provided counsel to represent *Big Table* and Mr. Joel J. Sprayregen, ACLU staff counsel, was appointed to the case.

I interrupted my reading to ask, "Aren't you glad you stuck with Joel Sprayregen as your attorney? I remember you said his lack of experience might scuttle the case."

"We were really lucky to have him on our side."

I continued reading,

> At the request of Big Table a Post Office
> Administrative hearing occurred in June,
> 1959 at the Main Post Office, Chicago.
> Among the distinguished men of letters
> and educators who testified either in
> person or by letter for the right of the
> people to receive *Big Table 1* through
> the mails were: Jacques Barzun, John
> Ciardi, Reverend Pierre Delattre,
> Lawrence Ferlinghetti, Allen Ginsberg,
> Hans W. Mattick, Norman Mailer,
> Hoke Norris, Harold Taylor, Lionel
> Trilling, and Anthony C. West. Paul
> Carroll testified as the publisher of *Big
> Table.* The Post Office attorney,
> in turn, produced one letter
> denying the literary merit of *Big
> Table 1,* written by August Derleth
> of Sauk City, Wisconsin. The result
> of the hearing was that the Post

Office declared *Big Table 1* not
fit to go through the mail. *Big Table*
then filed suit in the United States
District Court of Chicago, charging
that the postal ban was unconstitutional
and that the issue was a legitimate
literary effort. Attorney Sprayregen's
brief was lucid, passionate, and learned
in the law. After five months Judge
Julius Hoffman delivered his verdict.
He found it unnecessary to rule on
the constitutionality of the Post Office
ban. Instead, Judge Hoffman held
that *Big Table 1* was not
"obscene." Commenting on the
two articles in *Big Table* singled out
by the Post Office as such
("Old Angel Midnight" by Jack Kerouac
and ten episodes from *Naked
Lunch* by William S. Burroughs) Judge
Hoffman ruled that both were in the
broad field of serious literature. The

Kerouac article was described by Judge Hoffman "as a wild prose picnic which seems to be some sort of dialogue, broadly, between God and Man." The Burroughs novel, he said, was intended to shock contemporary society in order perhaps to better point out its flaws and weaknesses. Judge Hoffman concluded his ruling

by quoting from the *Ulysses* decision: "Art certainly cannot advance under compulsion to traditional forms, and nothing in such a field is more stifling to progress than limitation of the right to experiment with a new technique.'

`"I know you were more than pleased with Judge Hoffman's decision in your case. You were relieved, after two years of anxiety regarding the reality of a jail sentence, legal fines and what would be the legacy of *Big Table*. What did you think of Judge Hoffman's proceedings in the Chicago Seven Trial ten years later?"

"Wow, what a difference! Of course all the individuals, the judge and the defendants, were openly insulting to each other. Thank God, my case didn't roll out the way that one did. But then, Judge Hoffman's judgments in the Chicago Seven case were all thrown out in the Appeals court."

"Paul, remember the time we visited the architect Walter Netsch and his wife, Dawn Clark Netsch, told us how she had clerked for Judge Hoffman in the late fifties? She thought she might have written the brief for your case. And do you also remember Muriel Kallis Newman's gossip about Judge Hoffman?"

"Yes, they both lived in the Drake Hotel Apartments, and she told us that when they were in the elevator together he would always turn to show his best aspect, his profile?"

"Paul, she also said he was short and looked a little like Mr. Magoo."

Paul turned his head slowly to the left and posed.

"Not my best feature, is it?" He paused briefly. "I'm exhausted. Remembering those weary times has sapped my old energy. It must have followed my teeth out of town. Let's go to bed. At least I have you to hug."

He cocked his closely shaven head as he finished his

wine, and asks me, "What do you hear, dear? Is that coyotes? Is it someone's hunting dogs? I bet Stanley's out hunting with his coon dogs."

"Well, as long as he doesn't shoot our way."

"Oh, Stanley won't shoot at all. It's practice for timed competition with his hounds."

"Late at night, Paul? Practicing in the woods? I think it's crazy to be out in the woods at night, following dogs."

"Yes, and you didn't grow up here in the Appalachian Mountains like Stanley's clan, which has lived here since before the Civil War."

As I shake my head in amusement, I take Paul's arm and we make our way back to the house illuminated by the moon.

Thicker than Blood

"Paul, this morning, walking up to the horse barn, I felt very sharp, biting cold air. But the sun was so bright and clear glistening on the snow, it was as though someone had strewn diamonds across it. Absolutely beautiful! Did you see it from your window?"

"I wish I had but I wasn't feeling well."

"That's it. We're not going outside tonight. It might be our last chance until spring, but it's freezing."

"C'mon, honey, are you afraid I'll catch cold? I have cancer! I'm beginning to feel like I'm in jail!"

"You know all those stories you have to tell me? You can't do it sick in bed. Do you know how fortunate you are that you haven't had any pain?"

"Not yet, anyway. You win. I can't carry out the wine tray. We'll have to sit in my study."

We were in Paul's room as the sun was starting to leave us. Gazing outside, like a prisoner through a cell window, he turned to me and read from his notepad the first draft of a poem:

UNTITLED

A surprise always
like seeing an angel naked. So sudden
like a kid blurting out a truth
this quick awareness of the world around you
as if anything at all you see
is a Christmas present you never ever thought you'd get
like 50 years ago
running around the farm at Palos Park
looking
like a lover
at cowpie or a chicken
or icon of a locust husk.

"I like it, Paul! Naked angel to locust husk. It was your childhood history on the farm that made me think moving here might be good for both of us."

"I know. I thought of those memories when you talked me into it. Can you imagine me being carried down the spiral staircase at Ada Street as my illness advanced?"

"Ada Street is long gone. Back to *Big Table*. I'm still wondering about all the reasons why you stopped publishing it. The magazine, I mean. Wasn't it selling well?"

"It was a hot potato. As I told you, it had the largest circulation of any little magazine in its day; average copies per issue were 7,500, with the largest print run of 10,000 copies for the first two issues. But that didn't mean there was a profit."

"So, what were the reasons you stopped its publication? I know that Allen Ginsberg was browbeating you into accepting his poets, John Weiners, Raymond Bremser. Was it the lack of appreciation of your own poetry, or all the money it cost for the court reporter to cover the Post Office trial as well as the constant time it demanded keeping you from writing your poetry?"

"Yeh, Allen was pushing Weiners, a student of Charles Olson at Black Mountain College. He even sent me tapes of Weiners's reading! I couldn't appreciate either him, Ray Bremser or Olson. Also, the financial hassle was wearing me out – as well as the hostility from the press and friends like Isabella Gardner, and her husband, Allen Tate. But mostly I wanted time for my own writing. I believed I had only 35 years left and I wanted to see how my work could develop if I invested some care and time."

"So what did Isabella Gardner and Allen Tate say about your editing of *Big Table*?"

"My dear buddy Isabella had unfortunately married Allen Tate in 1959. They wrote to me saying they couldn't understand why I would be involved in such 'rabble; such uncivilized writing,' in response to my sending them *Big Table 1*.

"'Well,' I wrote her in reply to their criticism, 'We are at loggerheads about what is genuine and valuable among the new poets. Disagreement is natural and doesn't hurt: what does hurt is the assumption behind your tone of voice, dear Isabella, that somehow I am hypocritical and lack, as your husband so smugly and pretentiously put it, "editorial integrity."'

"I told them that 'I refuse to think that just because Allen Ginsberg, for example, is an exhibitionist and in many ways a psychotic and vulgar man, I refuse to think that this makes him a bad poet, when, in truth, my sensibility tells me that some of his verse has moved me deeply and, on occasion, moved me to tears. Nor will I allow Ginsberg's dislike and lack of appreciation of my own verse and suspicion of me as a man because I can get out a magazine without having to beg from mother or foundation or university or publishing house; I will not allow this to cloud my judgment of his own work.

"'On the other hand, I do not print Bill Merwin because he has been crowned with laurel and is considered by many to be the most accomplished poet of his generation. I print Merwin and Ginsberg because I believe the poems of theirs I have chosen are good poems. It is as simple as that.'

"'Finally,' I told them, 'I leave literary politics to your husband and to Ginsberg and to whoever gets his kicks out of playing such a cheap and crafty game.'"

"Boy, that's telling them! So they ganged up on you over publishing the Beats. Didn't you later resume your friendship with them?"

"Absolutely! Belle and I were family. We continued our constant correspondence for years. I mistakenly continued to think of Allen as a friend while he sabotaged my career. I asked him for a letter in support of my candidacy for the Yale Younger Poet's Award.

"Blast it! I received his damning letter too late. It had already gone to their advisory board.

"Then Robert Lowell, another 'friend,' gave a damaging reader's review of my work when I was about to have a volume of poetry published by Holt, Rinehart and Winston."

"But, Paul, how do you know that?"

"My cousin, Marie, worked as an editor with them. She did research in their files.

"The worst turn of the screw was how Allen broke Belle's heart. They had been married for several years when she went to Yaddo as a visiting writer. That was when Allen left her for an even younger woman, a student and former nun. Belle was brokenhearted. She had mostly abandoned her writing because he asked her to. Now he just dumped her. I tried to console and support her all I could with my letters. Isn't it ironic that she wrote: 'If there is a theme with which I am particularly concerned, it is the contemporary failure of love.'"

"Paul, I never met Isabella or Tate, although I remember answering the phone at three a.m. when she was calling from the Chelsea Hotel to chat. They're part of your first poetry circle, before the Beats, aren't they?"

"Isabella was my first poet friend, she was family:

sister, mother. She was the only woman I included in my book *The Poem In Its Skin*. Most of the male poets became famous, John Ashbery, Robert Creeley, James Dickey, Allen Ginsberg, and W. S. Merwin.

"I always believed that Belle was a fine poet. I thought 'The Widow's Yard' shared with Frost's 'Mending Wall' a slyness in the words of the first voice – that of a woman visiting her neighbor who has just become a widow. What I mean is that while we think she is acting charitably to the woman, where is the proof of kindness in her words? Instead of condolence, she offers a lecture on snails.

"In 'Mending Wall,' Frost gives us the impression the speaker is smarter than his neighbor, not traditional enough to insist on the rite of spring fence mending. Actually he, not his neighbor, is the one who brings up the subject. In both poems we have a narrator about whom we have to ask, do we trust this person? Does this ring a bell with you?"

"Paul, you know as well as I that a poet surfs on a wave of creativity without fully intuiting the message emerging on the page. When did you meet Isabella?"

"In 1952 when I visited the office of *Poetry* magazine. They were on the University of Chicago campus at that time.

"I was looking for Karl Shapiro, a Poet Laureate of the Library of Congress and a straight-shooting poet. Not unlike the Beats, Karl thought that form in poetry was not as important as feeling. He later told me he had asked himself what he would have done with 'Howl.' He left *Poetry* magazine just at the time *Howl and Other Poems* was about to be published. He said he was a great admirer of it but if Ginsberg had given him that poem, he didn't know if he would have put his life on the line.

"But Karl was not there that day in 1952. Behind a desk topped with mountains of manuscripts was his associate editor, Isabella. She and I took to each other like we were family. After all, we were both born to wealth (she still had oodles). We both loved literature and she was a good-looking redhead eager to discuss poetry.

"At that time she was married to Bob McCormick, of the McCormick reaper and *Chicago Tribune* money, and lived in a spiffy house in Elmhurst, designed by Mies van der Rohe. It is now part of the Elmhurst Art Museum.

After she married Allen Tate in 1959, she and Allen were my introduction to some of the Fugitives."

"Fugitives from what?"

"From the North and certainly from industrialization. Tate had been part of a group of Southern poets. He, John Crowe Ransom, Cal Lowell, and I occasionally hung out together before my association with the Beats. These early poet pals were at the opposite end in style and manner to the Beats. "This notebook came from those days."

He hands me an old notebook, spiral bound, six by nine inches, lined yellow paper with such notes and translations from Latin as this:

> Hesterno fetere mero qui credit Acerram,
> fallitur.
> In lucern semper Acerra bitit.

Then Paul's translation:

> He's dead wrong, whoever believes Acerra
> reeks of yesterday's wine:
> Acerra souses always into tomorrow.

"Paul, this has nothing to do with Beat poetry."

"Right on! It's pre-Beat by about two thousand years. Imagine this scene, honey: the Quadrangle Club on the University of Chicago's campus, with oak-paneled walls, white-jacketed, gloved waiters serving sherry, and all of us, John Crowe Ransom, Allen Tate, Robert Lowell, and myself dressed in three-piece tweeds reciting from memory lines of poetry in Latin. Isabella Gardner was my introduction. But, of course, as a woman she wasn't present, even though Robert Lowell was her cousin and Tate would become her fourth husband.

"Ransom, the oldest, the leader, reminded me of my father. He had a quiet natural authority. Lowell was almost Belle's age and ten years older than me. Ransom had taught Tate, a Poet Laureate of the Library of Congress (1943–44). Tate had taught Lowell, also a Poet Laureate (1947–48)."

"I've got it. The good old boys' club, the image and the lineage."

"They all talked New Criticism, a rigorous critical theory of literature, exactly the doctrine I was taught at the University of Chicago before I met them. New Criticism had a tight focus. It was a strict reading of the text, asking the reader to forgo biographical and other 'extraneous' investigation. While I listened carefully to both my university teachers and John Crowe Ransom, I found myself irresistibly drawn to library stacks so I could hunt down random bits of information about poets.

"My taste was the same as when I was searching out juicy lines from *Ulysses*. In the course of this schoolboy study I would find delectable bits of information, sticky sweet, such as Lord Byron's Greek mistress, a laundress who threw him down the stairs.

"I always felt that if information was true, why not know it? Should I continue my lecture? You look sleepy."

"Absolutely! I'm all ears."

"Well, Robert Lowell had his own digression from New Criticism when, in 1959, he published *Life Studies*, a confessional volume of poems. His style wasn't Ginsbergian, but they were both using poetry as a means to confess."

"Paul, I always thought New Criticism's formal approach had similarities to Clement Greenberg's Formalist theories of art, even though they had spawned such offspring as Jackson Pollock's all-over drip paintings, like those on Muriel Kallis Newman's walls. Pollock's paintings, with their avant-garde wildness and focus on the unconscious, seemed closer in nature to the literature of the Beats."

"Yes, but the transition from the Fugitives to 'Howl' was like jumping out the window from an academic afternoon of sipping sherry into an evening in a dark West Coast bar with poetry readings.

"There were some ironic elements of humor in that austere group of Southern poets. Cal Lowell was not Southern, he was from Boston, like Belle. But he reverted to being a schoolboy at Vanderbilt in the presence of his teachers, even though he was a Poet Laureate of Congress. He would affect a southern accent and Ransom would dole out assignments to him. 'Cal, you really should read the early poems of Sextus Propertius' (in Latin, of course).

"I think the highly structured form of my 1959 poem 'Winter Scene' was influenced by my contact with these men. Just as I know Ginsberg and the Beats influenced my later work.

"Belle and I, as family, were always trying to help each other. I would write to her of my love and intention to marry Inara, my ongoing psychoanalysis, my current poems, and the frustrating inability I continually experienced to get a poetry volume published. I was the only poet of my colleagues who hadn't achieved this. My desk was groaning under a stack of rejections.

"Like a mother or father reaches out to a wounded child, Belle offered to organize a group of friends who would finance the publication of my poems. I wouldn't hear of it, although I deeply appreciated her sympathy and efforts to help. If my own mother had been as caring as Belle, perhaps I wouldn't have spent so much time in analysis."

"Paul, I knew your mother. But tell me what you mean."

"When I was fourteen, Mother took me to an ancient doctor who diagnosed me as having TB. No second opinion was sought. After I spent four months of internment with old men in bathrobes spitting and coughing, the doctors at the TB sanatorium released me because a new x-ray showed no spots. This happened the year my father began his four-year-long death march with colon cancer."

"Paul, that's awful."

While we were sitting, sipping, talking, we saw snow silently steadily falling. Suddenly we heard a crash. Outside the window the beautiful star magnolia tree has lost one of its branches, split through by its burden of snow.

Saul Bellow

While washing dishes I glanced through the window at the yellow grace of early daffodils. These were precious gifts from the widow who lived here before us. Neighbors tell me when they see flowers still blooming around the house they remember Rachel.

Daffodils and, maybe, spring weather? Possibly we can return to our creek-side ritual. Housebound for three months now, Paul is crankily answering questions for Annie, his hospice nurse. I hug Annie before she leaves. Then I hug Paul noticing again the more-meager meat on his ribs. Six months of dueling with cancer can be felt. Yet Paul can walk without help. A stranger might never guess his illness.

"I think it's warm enough for us to go outside, Paul."

"About time! I was wondering when somebody would hear my prayers. And I have a new poem, 'Last Will & Testament.' Would you read it to me? I want to hear how it sounds when spoken."

"Of course. Let me get our drinks." After I get the wine, Paul follows me outside. I wipe the moisture and a dead ladybug off his chair. After our winter exile we once again resume sitting by the creek.

"Ah, finally, the creek's music again. The air even smells of spring. I'm ready, Posie. Go ahead."

I start to read:

LAST WILL & TESTAMENT

To the turkey buzzards of Beaver Dam Road

I will my eyes

May they help them see the secrets of the night

To the clouds above Jake Eggers's farm today

I will these hands to help them make their masks

To anyone who lives for the odors of the season

I will my nose

And to these innumerable ladybugs all about our porch this fall

I will my skin

in the event they need a winter coat

To Maryrose

I will my heart

where it has always been

To my son Luke

I will what brains there are inside my skull

especially these that look like streets that twist and turn on
    which the

poets walk and the inhabitants of the Dublin of Ulysses

To anyone who wants to flee bigotry and superstition
I will my feet
And to Senator Jesse Helms of North Carolina
I will my bowels
shaped like oversized tobacco leaves

"Ah, Paul, what a combination of sorrowful, generous, humorous thoughts. Incredible! I am so glad I have always had your heart! I can hear it beat.

"Your 'Last Will & Testament' reminds me of the fifteenth-century French poet François Villon. You told me about his lamenting on where are the snows of yesteryear and he goes on to name various women now gone, from Joan of Arc to Big Foot Bertha.

"Do you remember a spring of yesteryear, in Chicago, when for some reason we were walking west – down Fullerton Avenue with our favorite author, Saul Bellow? Passing bungalows not unlike those in Humboldt Park, where he grew up, Saul was telling us it was here, during the Depression, that the smell of bathtub gin and sauerkraut filled the air. I heard him say he found his memory of the past was as powerful, and as clear, as the present.

"Paul, when I first met him at an Art Institute reception, he was in his sixties, spry, very witty; dressed in a mix of academic and racetrack tout style, with a slightly cocked fedora. He told me that to prepare for writing he would stand on his head and drink gin. He was comic, but not a prankster, so I believed him."

"Posie, I don't think I told you Saul was one of the judges for the Longview Literary Awards for work in the first two issues of *Big Table*? After all the controversy and censorship, receiving those awards was like a big hug, like a Good Housekeeping stamp of approval. One award went to William S. Burroughs, for ten episodes from *Naked Lunch*, another went to Gregory Corso, *Three Poems*, both in *Big Table* 1. And the third to Edward Dahlberg, *Because I Was Flesh*, Part One, in *Big Table* 2.

"Saul also was a great help when I went to ask his advice, in 1967. I had considerable experience teaching at Notre Dame, the University of Chicago, Loyola, the Program in Creative Writing at the University of Iowa, and Branford College at Yale. All fine and good, but provisional. I wanted a *good* teaching job. Something permanent. My analyst, a dictatorial woman, was hounding me to go back to school and get a PhD. Saul was kind enough to meet me and offer advice. He told me very bluntly, but warmly, 'Screw the PhD. Do it through literature. You already have a good start. Get your books out and they will begin asking you.' I liked him a lot.

"Two years later, I had achieved three printings for *The Poem In Its Skin*, four for *The Young American Poets*, with a review in *Time* magazine. I arranged for the young poets to read at the New York lofts of Robert Rauschenberg, Jasper Johns and Red Grooms. I also wrote interviews with Norman Mailer, Allen Ginsberg and a profile of Andy Warhol – all published in *Playboy* magazine.

"In 1969 I was offered a full professorship in English at the University of Illinois at Chicago. Three years before I met you I founded the Program for Writers, the school's graduate program for creative writing, in 1974.

"Saul had hit it right on the nose! I had a secure future."

"I remember how generously he accepted the invitation to meet your class in 1990. You were teaching a class focused on *Humboldt's Gift*. With a request granted to change the time of the meeting '(as Saul said, 'not even Scriabin can sing before 10 a.m.,) he graciously accepted, and we chauffeured him and his fifth wife, Janice Bellow, to campus. After he spoke and answered student questions, I asked one which he said he enjoyed: 'Given your aptitude for careful observation of humans, do you consider our collective behavior has changed since you were young?'

"'Absolutely,' he said. 'When I was young we had individual thinkers. We called them eccentric. Today, I think we come to decisions mainly through consensus.' I had not read his 1976 Nobel speech at that time. Now, having done so, I know my question got to the heart of his speech, without mentioning Alain Robbe-Grillet.

"And Paul, do you remember the second party we threw for Saul in 1985? He said he wanted to meet local writers. His Hyde Park apartment was much smaller than our loft. Do you remember the end of the party?"

"Just slightly."

"The last to leave that night were Saul and Alexandra, his fourth wife, a Romanian math professor. As she descended our spiral staircase in her red dress and shoes, Saul mused about his youth 'when young men would play hooky, go to the corner of State and Van Buren Streets, and watch the burlesque performers descend in their robes down the fire escape, from their dressing rooms to the oyster bar below.'"

"It's coming back to me. It was a fun party."

"You know I was not the only woman in Chicago to note and enjoy the attentive and complimentary way Saul's eyes would actively follow us. He was persistently polite, never a challenge like Jim Dickey. But I may have been one of only a few who realized his interest in mysticism. He studied and mentioned Rudolf Steiner in Humboldt's Gift. I was interested to read there:

> therefore I am obliged to deny that so
> extraordinary a thing as a human soul can
> be wiped out forever. No, the dead are about
> us, shut out by our metaphysical denial of
> them. As we lie nightly in our hemisphere,
> asleep by the billions our dead approach
> us. Our ideas should be their nourishment.
> We are the grainfields. But we are barren

and we starve them. Don't kid yourself,

though, we are watched by the dead, watched

on this earth, which is our school of freedom.

[p.141]

"Paul, I wish Saul were watching me tonight and could tell me whether he named his character Humboldt because he had grown up in Humboldt Park."

"I told you Humboldt was based on Delmore Schwartz. His parents, like Saul's, came from Romania."

"Do you remember the funny story he told us about the Nobel Prize ceremonies?"

"Sure, Posie, you mean when the Swedish vestal virgins with crowns of bright burning candles burst unannounced into their bedroom?"

"Paul, he didn't say whether he and Alexandra were just surprised or terribly embarrassed."

"Honey, we're going to need candles ourselves if we don't head inside. It's getting too sensual and dark out here."

"Just take my hand, Paul."

Dedication of *The Column on the Pond*

I am driving Paul ninety miles to Charlotte for the dedication of my sculpture in mid-June 1996. I don't know that he has only ten more weeks to live. Cancer has whittled him down to a stick-like figure, walking stiffly, but he is eager to read his poems before today's audience. One of his poems circles the base of my sculpture. Gliding under bright blue sky with a few fluffy slowly moving clouds we see the skyscrapers of Charlotte come into view.

I was on this route alone two weeks before, driving a twenty-four-foot Great Hauler rental truck. Friends had helped me load sculpture parts into the truck at an angle, over the cab back to the lift door, to fit them into the truck. Once installed, the assembled sculpture will stand twenty-eight feet tall. We tie individual "stems with leaves" to horizontal wood rails, ensuring all these sections will arrive safely.

I was scared during that earlier trip, just as I always am when erecting sculpture. I never know what might happen. Once, in Springfield, Illinois, the building engineer and I miscalculated the swing distance necessary to move a twenty-three-foot base through the hallway, turn a corner, and arrive at the building's atrium. It wouldn't fit through. As a result, twelve feet of steel wall studding had to be cut to allow the passage of the base. That done, employees of the *Illinois Journal-Register* newspaper, standing on two floors of balconies surrounding the atrium sculpture site, had to haul with ropes to lift the base upright because the skylight above the atrium hadn't been engineered to hold the weight of the sculpture. So we couldn't use a hoist. I felt like we were actors in a Cecil B. DeMille movie, moving blocks to make a pyramid. This was just the start of the installation adventures for the forty-five-foot-tall *Lincoln Tree*.

I won this North Carolina commission, *The Column on the Pond*, through the Arts and Science Council of Charlotte, but I had no question who on the selection committee had selected me. Jake Jacobsen, managing a Mecklenburg County Social Services Department yearly budget of $350,000,000, had worries that governmental budget cuts might provoke bomb threats on the department's campus. He wanted a sculpture to cause his clients "to look up and be inspired."

When I arrived for the installation, members of

Mecklenburg County's maintenance crew were waiting to help. First we bolted the aluminum base to the concrete foundation. It was my friend Wilbur Tuggle, a structural engineer, who helped me design the base, allowing the sculpture to present the illusion that it is standing with little support. Jake wrote that "it is an aluminum-sound sculpture, standing more than 28 feet high, and is a blue circular ring of columns that divides into smaller twining branches and leaves. Wind chimes placed inside the columns resonate, soothing and charming visitors." It also has Paul's poem on the base circling the ring of columns:

ODE TO ST. MARY-OF-THE-WOODS COLLEGE
We can have stars

on the roofs of our mouths

whenever we care to have them there.

This poem was written in Terre Haute, Indiana, when Paul was on that campus to give a reading and was walking with a friend at night. They heard singing. Paul asked what was the source and his friend told him the music came from a house for retired nuns. Today as we near Charlotte, the weather is perfect.

As we arrive we see a crowd gathering. On the plateau opposite the sculpture site there is a decorated podium bearing a large seal of Mecklenburg County. Sound equipment and rows of seats have been set up. Men with news cameras and a Mecklenburg County video crew are waiting. Jake, the MC, soon goes to the podium and begins by noting that Ella Fitzgerald has just died and how her lyrics "How High the Sky" could be the theme for the sculpture. He introduces some politicians who kid around that if there isn't enough wind to cause the sculpture to sound, they are perfectly capable of providing hot air.

I speak briefly but amuse the audience about how during the installation three enthusiastic boys came running up to the sculpture. Soon their mother called to them to get going. Before they reluctantly left, they turned to me, high in the sculpture, and asked, "Will this still be here when we get back?" And I said, "It better be."

Then Jake introduces Paul. He first reads the poem that is on the sculpture, then a new one on the subject of poetry. As he often does, Paul interrupts the latter poem with commentary that occurred to him as he reads. He's as insouciant as ever, and strong on the power of poems to speak to, and for, everyone. At the end of the ceremonies, while ice cream is served, one of the social workers approaches Paul and asks, "Will you be back next week?" I could see disappointment on her face when he said no. He might be dying of cancer but he is still a charmer.

It is a wonderful day only slightly stained by getting a ticket in Yadkin County's speed trap on our way home.

The Inn of the Poets in the Clouds

The rain is pounding outside, drumming like a marching band on our tin roof for over an hour. Lying in bed Paul can see the blooming star magnolia tree through a window, its multiple petals, long, narrow and curving, pushed toward the ground by the rain's weight. Such a tortured beauty. We don't need more rain. The water table is already high.

Moving to Paul's side I show him a cardboard box marked WFMT on the outside in black ink. It's full of cassette tapes from the radio station.

"Paul, you remember what good old George Drury sent us? He saved these from WFMT's office move in 1995. Here they all are, or maybe all of your *Name and Nature of Poetry* radio programs. George was worried they would be lost in the moving mess.

"You look tired, honey. Stay in bed. I'll bring over the cassette recorder and we can listen to one you would like to hear. There are seventy-five tapes here. I'm sure some have been lost. I remember you broadcast once a month for eight years. Here's the first, on A. E. Housman. You told me it was his lecture at Cambridge in 1933 that named your program."

Paul is silently nodding his head.

As the tape plays we hear Paul's old voice, not his currently feeble and cancer-diminished sound. Through a scratchy background noise we hear him speaking confidently, enthusiastically telling how that formidable Victorian scholar said, "if a line of poetry strays into my memory, my skin bristles so that the razor ceases to act."

Paul whispers that his lucky charm while recording was a Xerox of a *Punch* cartoon showing an elderly Housman playing flute music to a Grecian muse in a temple. The muse extends her arms to welcome him. It was dated October 1922, when Housman had broken his silence and published his. Eventually, Paul tells me, he replaced the temple with his radio broadcast of "The Inn of the Poets in the Clouds."

"Where was the inn located?"

He whispers that it started as a "pleasant, rather vague fantasy. It was somewhere over Lake Michigan." Listening, leaning together, we hear that the inn has Dickensian architecture with the fantastic exception that, in large sections, one can see through the walls and ceiling.

Golden chandeliers with crystal prism pendants hang high above, anchored in night's darkness. The brilliant light from the moon and stars cascades down through the chandeliers' prisms, sending rainbow colors upon the assembly below.

An immense hearth fills one end of a great room with yellow and orange sparks crackling out from a fire. The mantel above is crowded with evergreen boughs, bows, red and white holly berries.

The crowd inside the inn is a polyglot mix of the shades of poets from all countries, all centuries. There are Lapland poets, pygmy poets. Constantine Cavafy is dancing in his native Greek dress of billowing white sleeves and skirt with an azure blue and gold vest. Frederico García Lorca is decked out in a bullfighter's suit of lights with golden flowers embroidered on his sleeves. Publius Ovidius Naso and Miss Sara Teasdale of St. Louis, Missouri, are reciting verses to each other. She tells Ovid a joke, which spreads like ripples outward through the entire company, until all are lending their peals of laughter. The musicians rotate from drums and whistles to fiddles while the happy company joins in singing "Down by the Sally

Gardens." Then a waltz issues forth while Walt Whitman and Emily Dickinson, in white linen attire, circle round and round. Sparkling between the dancers, almost as another partner, is the rainbow light descending from the chandeliers. At a break, Persian musicians appear, their music introducing Shams of Tabriz, who begins a slow, hypnotizing Sufi twirling, casting a spell of quiet peace on the assembly.

It is an inn of joy, gaiety, and voices ringing with a multitude of verses in various languages. Through this great room Shakespeare and Rumi are ceaselessly moving, pouring wine from golden pitchers.

There are tables groaning with carved roast, turkey, and duck. Platters with potatoes, vegetables, shepherd's pie. There is no shortage of cakes, pies, puddings, tarts and all manner of sweet concoctions. It is a visual, olfactory glory of a feast, but not intended for consumption. All those assembled in the room are spirits with no material needs. These culinary treasures are placed to evoke the delicious memories of all the joys the gathered band of spirits had enjoyed in life.

In an upper room in the inn sit a few poets who are

missing out on the great party. They mistakenly think they were the only true, deserving poets laureate in this auspicious place. Too bad.

"Paul, I have sometimes wondered if I was reincarnated from Shams of Tabriz. Your notes, in *Poems & Psalms*, tell how Shams appeared in 1244, seven hundred years before my birth. Do you remember how, three years after we married, you stopped writing for a year saying you had intimations of a strange new poetry? And, when, after a year you resumed writing, the new poems were conversations with Shams. You've seen how, like a Sufi, I can spin endlessly without losing my balance."

I might have been asking a dreamer. Lying there in our bed Paul had lapsed into slow, frazzled breathing. I had called Luke the day before and could only hope he would arrive in time from Chicago.

It was Labor Day weekend, but fortunately Anne, Paul's hospice nurse, lived only one ridge over. She responded to my call and arrived in an hour with a morphine patch. Thank God, she overrode Dr. DeVirgilis' order for a drip feed so we wouldn't have to worry about a needle that might pull out when Paul tossed around in bed.

The next morning my neighbor Grace stayed with Paul while I drove to Boone and picked up Luke, who had flown down from Chicago. Like his father, he is tall, but with a mop of auburn curls. I described his dad's condition as we drove over George's Gap to the farm. Arriving, we went straight to Paul. After I thanked Grace for her help, we took up our vigil by the bed. Now Paul did not lapse from his sleeplike state. He lay there, still breathing, but rarely moving.

All we could do was wait. Luke and I didn't know if Paul could hear us. Through the morning, until three in the afternoon, when the earth's energy was in a low phase, we watched him breathe slower, more slowly. We couldn't see any color in his face. Then the moment came when we thought everything had stopped. Looking closely, we checked to see if any breath was still coming. It wasn't. I felt cleft in half, but there was no pain. I was just numb. Luke and I grabbed and hugged each other, crying.

Six Months Later

A fine February morning in the mountains, sunlight streaming through my yoga teacher Joanne's window, a prism casting lively rainbows across the room as we sidestep, loosening our bodies before yoga class begins. Despite consoling from hospice ladies, I have chosen yoga instead of the grieving class offered by Hospice. I decided my body rather than mind was the path to peace. Suddenly, my teacher Joanne halts her stretching. She looks up at me and asks:

"Where is everyone? At least five said they would be here today."

"I don't see them."

Joanne shakes her head, dark curls swinging, "Tell me, Maryrose, have you been dreaming again of Paul?"

I paused, tears suddenly welling. "Yes, yes, I have, I am. I think he wants me…wants me…to move his ashes."

Joanne silently rises, retrieves a crystal from a collection in her bedroom, and returns to the room, slowly sitting down while holding the crystal against her throat.

"No, I don't think that is his intention," she says slowly, eyes shut. Suddenly, she speaks and it is as if she begins to speak for Paul. "He has been with a group somewhere, and they are working together on their individual problems and to save the earth. He has chosen to leave them to come here today to see you."

During my lonely grieving, sitting in a large old drafty farmhouse, I sometimes felt I could sense Paul's presence. Now, though thrilled to hear her words, I feel a twinge of fear. But who could have guessed or imagined what would now happen? In the next instant, I see a sphere of light in the room, glowing white and fuchsia. Is this Paul's spirit? Is Paul now light energy? How am I supposed to understand what's happening? This brilliant image stays briefly and then vanishes. Although Joanne didn't see this light image, as I did, I notice she's intent on something, her eyes closed as if she is carefully listening. Then she exclaims:

"He wants to leave here with you, right now!"

She and I grab each other, crying. What's happened is beyond anything we have ever experienced or dreamed of. Then, acting on her words, I – or, Paul and myself, we both – are leaving her house, when I remember Paul had told me the meaning of a slang expression from his Navy days. When a sailor said "he had his ashes hauled," that meant having sex. How amazing, I thought, desire might exist even in the afterlife. It was marvelous but strange. Could Paul travel, filled with fuchsia-colored desire, from somewhere, back to see me? Once he'd written to me in a poem: "You are where I belong!"

A Preface for Paul

Paul Carroll was a good friend, a firm friend, and old friend whom I never knew very well. My first impression of him was of a great horse, heavy-footed, but light in the eyes...I had a great liking for him, a great affection. He had poetic integrity, and he had integrity and courage as an editor -- one of the great counter-culture poetry editors. He had a kind of carnivorous imagination and a salty Catholic humor. (He liked jokes about the Pope's knuckles or other parts of the anatomy.)

I never saw him anywhere except in his Chicago, great Chicago. Three or four times he entertained me on his stomping grounds...after my reading at the original Barbara's Bookstore or at a *Big Table* reading early-on, in the sixties, no doubt...then at a big old German restaurant that he loved, in an old red brick building...Much later in his loft (warehouse studio) with his lovely Maryrose...

Then he disappeared into hinter America, I knew not where. He was gone when I read poetry last in Chicago, and I missed him, like part of Chicago was missing. I felt he should at least have left a note on a tree reading "Gone on" with an arrow pointing which way.

Now he *has* gone on – into some kind of avuncular poet's heaven or purgatorio. And all that's left of him is his poem, still here to shed special light on us – his complex inner light, his troubled light, his profoundly loving light, shining through the holes in his soul.

Lawrence Ferlinghetti, April 2000

POEMS & POEM FRAGMENTS
by PAUL CARROLL

SONG AFTER MAKING LOVE

Sometimes I want to be a cloud

drifting like a barnacle goose or a galleon

into the winter home of God

The green of these trees

the grass green as oxygen

the green of my excited heart

Shadows of birds between the bones

blood feels sweet as if moving in maple trees

      a part of me is grass

I close my eyes

I'm empty

at the same time full

like a galaxy in daylight

Maryrose Carroll

A VIRGILIAN MOON

Only the hint of the hump

Of a camel

The moon's become tonight

Behind a wall of cloud. When, suddenly,

It flashes half a face

But vanishes again

Like Dido in the other world, the clouds surrounding it

Turning into Oriental temple dragons, circles

Of Halloween yellow-and-brown

By some abstract expressionist, now like a pack

Of small stray dogs

Pursuing their own tails, a deer in flight. Abruptly,

The round moon blazes, white

As bone, alone

In a dark sky. The ancients were right -

The moon's a woman

And If I knew the words I'd pray to her tonight

In gratitude for my wife asleep

Whose body is another sky

Like the softness and the secrets of a summer's night.

Poems, 1988

FATHER

How sick
I get of your ghost.
And of always looking at this tintype on my desk
of you as a cocky kid:
Kilkenny's coast, rock and suncracked turf
giving the resilience to your countenance
as you try to seem so nonchalant, posing
in a rented Sunday morning suit
spats and bowler hat:
a greenhorn off the boat. And yet,
something in that twist of fist,
knuckles taut about the cane knob, shows
how you already seem to know
you'll transform that old cow pasture of Hyde Park
into your own oyster.

The way you did.

And that other photo
stuck somewhere in my dresser drawer
amid the Xmas handkerchiefs
the rubbers, poems
and busted rosary beads:
Posed beneath three palmtrees
on Tampa Beach's boardwalk,
a stocky man who'd made his millions by himself;
and could quarrel with Congressmen in Washington
about the New Deal bank acts;
or call Mayor Kelly crooked to his face.
Hair
bone, cock,

face and skin, brains:
rotten in the earth these 16 years.

        Remember, father, how Monsignor Shannon
        (whose mouth you always said
        looked exactly like a turkey's ass)
boomed out Latin above your coffin at Mount Olivet?
           But as the raw October rain
           rasped against our limousine
             guiding   the   creeping   cars   back   into
      Chicago.
    Jack, your first-born,
    picked his nose; and
    for an instant flicked a look
to ask if I too knew you were dead for good –
          St. Patrick's paradise a club
          for priests and politicians
          you wouldn't get caught dead in.

      You used to call me Bill.
And kiss me. Take me to the Brookfield Zoo.
    Or stuff English toffee in my mouth.
But always after you'd cursed
    and with a bedroom slipper
whacked the tar out of Jack.

        This morning, father,
        broke as usual,
        no woman in my bed,
    I threw six bucks away
    for a shave and haircut at The Drake.
And looked again for you.
          On Oak Street beach,

gazing beyond the bathers and the boats,
I suddenly searched the horizon, father,
            For that old snapshot of Picasso
                  and his woman Dora Maar.
            Picasso bald and 60;
but both in exaltation, emerging
                  with incredible sexual dignity
            from the waters of the Gulfe Juan.

                      Tattoo
                      of light
                      on lake.

            Bleached spine of fish.
Those ripple of foam: semen of the ghost.

                  I left the lake;
          but tripped in the quick dark
          of the Division Street underpass;
then picked a way past newspaper scraps,
                puddles and a puckered beachball.
          I looked for dirty drawings on the wall.
      Traffic crunches overhead.
This underpass is endless.

Odes, 1969; also published, in a slightly
different version, in The New American
Poetry, edited by Donald Allen, Grove Press,
NY, 1960.

GEORGE'S GAP

(George's Gap is a High Country area with twisting narrow road between Bethel Road and the village of Sugar Grove in Watauga County, North Carolina.)

The fog moves among the pine trees and the meadows far
    below like the breath of a god

I'm sitting here at the top of George's Gap

feeling I'm half cloud

with no more thought than what a fir tree has

The sea-green valleys and the pastures far below

have been here before the Cherokee

The land inside the soul is always green

The way these distant hills that look like buffalos

the trees and winter grass the tumbleweed about the road

and the caravan of clouds above

each contains a history

long as the history of the Jews

So any one of us

walking about downtown Boone today

that sprightly ASU student sporting a blue baseball cap turned
    backwards as a cue ball on green baize

and the Good Ol' Boy a block behind her with a pig-tail and
    battered lineman's boots he bought from Dan'l Boone

and the Sheriff's officer sauntering behind sinister black
    shades

even though today's as grey as the inside of an oyster

all carry a computer in the heart
that documents their history
as unique as the fingerprints of angels

The wind on George's Gap today is like a boxer
smashing the tall grass and the trees and me
as if we were pieces on a chessboard

The fog's begun to fade leaving
the brown grass
withered as an old man's mountain face
and the rows of tall stark trees naked as a baby after birth
Still even a plain person
is handsome when in love

Inching through thick fog in our 4x4 Jeep Cherokee
around these icy narrow twists and turns
a mile or two above the cattle and the earth below
you feel what it's like to be alive—
the armor of your pension
the health insurance policies with solid Medicare and Equicor
your belief in this or that
and the healthy happy love with Maryrose—
all evaporate within the fog

leaving you a man a million years ago

creeping on the Gap

not knowing if a god or dinosaur's around the bend

or if the road abruptly ends

in a black hole

A good art gallery or museum hangs a show

for a month or so

The show on George's Gap is different every day

Beaver Dam Road Poems, 1994

AN ORDINARY JANUARY DAY

A surprise always

Like seeing an angel naked. So sudden

Like a kid blurting out a truth

This quick awareness of the world around you

As if anything at all you see

Is a Christmas present you never ever thought you'd get

Like fifty years ago

running around the farm at Palos Park looking

like a lover

at cowpie or a chicken

or icon of a locust husk   Today

you're driving past Oz Park down Webster Avenue

an ordinary January day

an ordinary city park

suddenly the trees brown skeletons

look like Billy Bowlegs of the Seminoles

standing on his head for fun

the brown and pale green grass

a color Cezanne could have captured on canvas.

PSALM 2

I knew a man once who lived on the street of the

glassblowers in Damascus.

Who had his poems tattooed on his body.

There are many ways. As many

As the shadows of the ostriches

Flickering in the desert, at dusk, beyond the city's gates.

Take the pilgrim in this old woodcut –

He appears about to leave the meadow with its thistles,

the cattle of the Hebrews and the pond

Of cattails, an ordinary day in May; and move

Into another world beyond our own

With its seraglio of suns that also glow at night,

Every star a work of art.

Think of the pilgrim as having finished writing a new book,

Like you; yet, like you troubled by

Intimations of a kind of poetry

He's never written yet.

And maybe cannot ever write – where a word can contain

A midnight sky in spring,

Its tender silences;

Or be an amulet depicting the beehive of the sacred bees

Of death

All we can do is to wait and watch

For the flight of the gray storks that bring the rains with

them. Think now:

The poems may be in the meadow, after all.

They must come from a part of the heart

Where you have never been. Those stars may be as exquisite

As what's behind the masks the angels wear.

Forget them. Let the meadow be.

Poems & Psalms, 1990

TO MARYROSE

Clear, crisp,

bouncy, bountiful, all day,

gold-white the light,

elegant Ralph Guillaume pitching pigskins for the Irish,

the balloon man with foot of the goat

is back among us in the month of May,

that lassie in trenchcoat like an hourglass

a catalyst who conjures my honey here among

the press of passengers

bound for the Congress-Milwaukee B Train on the CTA.

My angel's eyes are Irish

light upon a lake:

and fun. Her black hair

the Rhineland meadow Meister Eckhart moves in.

I feel married to you, Maryrose. That's

it.

New and Selected Poems, 1977

SMALL HASIDIC SONG
(for a 59th birthday)

A priest with white Palm Beach summer straw

Is carrying the calendar away

forever, inside his leather brief case, walking

from the Cardinal's Florentine front door

at State Parkway and North Avenue.

The clouds too have disappeared today. No,

they've only come to earth

to become the cool shadows of the maple and the elms

here where Lincoln Park begins,

amid the elegant, small shadows

cast by the distant row of trees

slim as antlers of Pere David's deer.

It must be so—

we're all the ages that we ever were

because all I'm hearing here

is the quiet choir of the bumblebees

Circling around their brown cathedral

On the farm at Palos Park when I am ten.

Ah, if only I had paid attention

In Miss Kush's 8th grade dancing class

I might be able, now

To dance all day in the palm of God.

Poems, 1988

SYMPHONY IN WHITE, NO. 1

I didn't even need to buy a postcard of your
    painting
Leaving the National Gallery that day in 1953
After having stepped into your room by chance
    and
Suddenly the sluices
Opened in some dam within
Flooding me with your loveliness
I knew would be with me always.
The way it has.   The copperyred dark hair
Cascading down your shoulders
Looking like black cedars in sunset near the river
    in December.   And the eyes—
Like the first time
One looks into the sky at night and knows
The piercing of a sense of wonder
For which there is no name.
If you'd been naked. Jo, I never would have left
that room alive.

        The Garden of Earthly Delights, 1985

POEM TO A NIGHT IN MAY

The silence in a night like this

Seems like the silence of an octopus

I want to live in it forever

Away from the hullabaloo of the daily

     traffic down Elston Avenue

And everywhere. And be silent with my soul

At the bottom of the sea

I doubt if it's a longing for the

     Silence of the womb   Rather

A longing for the face of God

That ocean full of stars

UNTITLED

If I could make a poem as mysterious

And simple as the sea

Its silent undulation like the creases in the palm of God

The blues and greens the colors of the words we try to find

When talking of a love that counts   Those

waves

Cracking against the rocks

Making endless works of art.

Then it might finally feel finished

The work that's been given me to do.

We come from the ocean.   And we return to it.

Our hands full of poems like prayers.

POEM FRAGMENT (NO NAME)

Sudden talk and laughter of invisible birds

Everywhere about me

Here on this path in the park

I love these times because they have no "meaning"

They are what they are. Like love.

Like thunder.

POEM FRAGMENT (NO NAME)

If earth were like a friend

Would we gouge and gash it

Poison and pollute it as we do?

We'd hang around it like a lover

And we'd know

This ladybug inching along the bench I'm sitting on

is more mysterious and elegant than diamonds.

POSTCARD
(From a Village near Caesarea Philippi in Palestine)

No one can be born for anybody else.

No one can smell the fresh acrid odor of the spring

Nor make love for anybody else.

No one can write anybody else's poem

Or tell them how to feel.

No one sees the stars the way one person sees them.

No one can die anybody else's death.

ANCESTRAL SONG

Who are we? Where do we come from? Where are
we going?

Only the wind knows

And the wind knows everything but has no tongue.

And what if God looks like a tree

Or the shadow of a crow

Or one of the fish that move inside our hearts.

The summer night has many voices. They seem to be
saying

We may be in heaven here.

There are stars beneath our skins

We can contain the universe within our skull.

Bibliography

Anderson, Elliot, and Mary Kinzie, eds. *The Little Magazine in America: A Modern Documentary History.* Yonkers, NY: Pushcart Press, 1978.

Bent, Jaap van der. "Beats on the Table: Beat Writing in the Chicago Review and Big Table." *TS: Tijdschrift voor tijdschriftstudies* [Magazine for Magazine Studies] no. 31 (June 2012): 5–19. http://www.tijdschriftstudies.nl/index/php/TS/article/view/URN:NBN:NL:UI:10-1-101668.

Big Table 1, ed. Irving Rosenthal and Paul Carroll. Big Table, Inc., Chicago, 1959.

Big Table 5, ed. Paul Carroll. Big Table, Inc, Chicago, 1960.

Birmingham, Jed. "William Burroughs and Norman Mailer." *Reality Studio: A William S Burroughs Community.* http://www.realitystudio.org/bibliographicbunker/william-burroughs-and-norman-mailer.

Brennan, Gerald E. "Big Table." *Chicago History: The Magazine of the Chicago Historical Society* 17, nos. 1–2 (Spring–Summer 1998): 4–23.

_____. "Big Table." *The Blacklisted Journalist*, Column Thirty-Nine, November 1, 1998. http://www.blacklistedjournalist.com/column39c.html

_____. "Naked Censorship: The True Story of the University of Chicago and William S. Burroughs's *Naked Lunch,* Part I." *Chicago Reader*, September 29, 1995, 17–18.

_____. "Naked Censorship: The True Story of the University of Chicago and William S. Burroughs's *Naked Lunch,* part II." *Chicago Reader*, October 6, 1995,

8–10, 12, 14, 16, 20, 22, 24–28.

Bruce, Glenn A. "A Life in Beat Poetics." *The Beat Poets of the Forever Generation.* http://thebeatspoetsoftheforevergenera.blogspot.com.

Campbell, James. *This Is the Beat Generation: New York, San Francisco, Paris.* Berkeley: University of California Press, 1999.

Carroll, Paul. *The Beaver Dam Road Poems.* Boone, NC: Big Table Books, 1994.

_____. *Chicago Tales.* Chicago: Big Table Books, 1991.

_____. *The Garden of Earthly Delights.* (Recipient of the 1985 Chicago Poets Award.) Chicago: Chicago Office of Fine Arts, Department of Cultural Affairs / Chicago Public Library, 1985.

_____. Interview with Allen Ginsberg. *Playboy* 16, no. 4 (April 1969): 81–92, 236–244.

_____. Interview with Norman Mailer. *Playboy* 15, no. 1 (January 1968): 69–84.

_____. Interviewed by John Logan. Tucson, AZ: Interview Press, 1966.

_____. Interviewed by Art Lange. *Brilliant Corners*, no. 7 (Fall 1977): 20–31.

_____. Letters to Isabella Gardner. Special Collections, Olin Library, Washington University Libraries, St. Louis, MO.

_____. *The Luke Poems.* Chicago: Big Table Publishing Company, 1971.

_____. *New and Selected Poems.* Chicago: Yellow Press, 1978.

_____. "New Year's Eve with a Dead Surrealist." *Chicago Review* 11, no. 4 (Winter 1958): 52 ff.

_____. "Notes on Some Young Poets." Fifty Years: A Retrospective Issue, *Chicago Review* 42, nos. 3–4 (Summer–Fall 1996): 31–33.

_____. *Odes.* Chicago: Big Table Publishing Company, 1969.

_____. "The Pentecostal Poems of *Kaddish*." In *On the Poetry of Allen Ginsberg*, edited by Lewis Hyde, 94–95. Ann Arbor: University of Michigan Press, 1984.

_____. *The Poem In Its Skin.* Chicago: Follett Publishing Company / A Big Table Book, 1968.

_____. *Poems.* Peoria, IL: Spoon River Poetry Press, 1988.

_____. *Poems & Psalms.* Chicago: Big Table Books, 1990.

_____. *Straight Poets I Have Known and Loved.* Boone, NC: Big Table Books, 1995

_____. *The Young American Poets.* Chicago: Follett Publishing Company / A Big Table Book, 1968.

Cold Mountain Review, ed. Leon Lewis, Spring 2008, Appalachian State University, Boone, NC. (Contains two poems by Paul Carroll and image of Maryrose Carroll's *Column on the Pond.)*

Dickey, Christopher. *Summer of Deliverance: A Memoir of Father and Son.* New York: Simon & Schuster, 1998.

Dickey, James. *Crux: the Letters of James Dickey*, edited by Judith S. Baughman. Knopf, 1999.

Gardner, Isabella. "Hospitality." *New York Review of Books,*

October 26, 1967.

http://www.nybooks.com/articles/archives/1967/oct/26
/hospitality-2/.

Ginsberg, Allen. "Big Table Reading, 1959" (Audio of
Ginsberg reading "Howl" and nine other poems at a
benefit reading for *Big Table* magazine held at the
Sherman House in Chicago on January 29, 1959.)
http://www.writing.upenn.edu/pennsound/x/Ginsberg.php.

_____. *Spontaneous Mind: Selected Interviews 1958–1996.* Edited
by David Carter. New York: HarperCollins, 2001.

Hoover, Paul. "On Paul Carroll." (Issue contains 4 poems by
Paul Carroll.) *Chicago Review* 44, no. 1 (1998): 5–12.

Janssen, Marianne. *Not at All What One Is Used To: The Life and
Times of Isabella Gardner.* Columbia, MO: University of
Missouri Press, 2010.

Johnson, Joyce. *The Voice Is All: The Lonely Victory of Jack
Kerouac.* New York: Viking, 2012.

Mayer, Milton. *Robert Maynard Hutchins: A Memoir.* Edited by
John H. Hicks. Berkeley: University of California Press,
1993.

McQuade, Molly, ed. *An Unsentimental Education: Writers and
Chicago.* Chicago: University of Chicago Press, 1995.

Morgan, Bill, and David Stanford, eds. *Jack Kerouac and Allen
Ginsberg: The Letters.* New York: Viking, 2010.

The Paul D. Carroll Papers 1950–1996. Special Collections
Research Center, University of Chicago Library. (See
"Guide to the Paul D. Carroll Papers 1950–1996" at
http://www.lib.uchicago.edu.)

The Paul and Maryrose Carroll Beat Collection, Special Collections at Belk Library, Appalachian State University, Boone, NC.

Poetry Center of Chicago. "About."
http://www.poetrycenter.org/about.

Poetry Foundation. "Biography" of Paul Carroll.
http://www.poetryfoundation.org/bio/paul-carroll.

Reddy, Srikanth, ed. *From Poetry to Verse: Essays on the Making of Modern Poetry*. Chicago: Special Collections Research Center, University of Chicago Library, 2005.

Other Big Table Books Published by Paul Carroll

Codrescu, Andrei. *License to Carry a Gun*. Volume 3 in the Big Table Series of Younger Poets. 1970.

Knott, Bill. *Auto-Necrophilia*. 1971.

_____. [Saint Geraud, pseud.]. *The Naomi Poems, Book One: Corpse and Beans*. Volume 1 in the Big Table Series of Younger Poets. 1968.

Norris, Kathleen. *Falling Off*. Volume 4 in the Big Table Series of Younger Poets. 1971.

Porchia, Antonio. *Voices*. Translated by W. S. Merwin. 1969.

Saroyan, Aram. *Words & Photographs*. 1970.

Schmitz, Dennis. *We Weep for Our Strangeness*. Volume 2 in the Big Table Series of Younger Poets. 1969